Historic Tales of
TERRITORIAL TUCSON
1854–1912

David Devine

THE History PRESS

Published by The History Press
Charleston, SC
www.historypress.com

Opposite: Jim Ayres (1936–2015) by Blake Higgins, 2008. *Marianne Ayres.*

First published 2020

Manufactured in the United States

ISBN 9781467145053

Library of Congress Control Number: 2020941953

For Jim Ayres, whose interest in Tucson history, historical research and preservation of historic structures was unparalleled.

CONTENTS

ACKNOWLEDGEMENTS

Jim Ayres had an avid interest in Tucson's Chinese community. As lead researcher on the city's downtown urban renewal archaeology project area from 1967 to 1979, he learned a great deal. But his curiosity continued. Having semi-retired around the year 2000, Jim began looking at early southern Arizona English-language newspapers on microfilm at the Arizona Historical Society to locate mentions of the Chinese.

This mind-numbing, eye-straining work was both tedious and frustrating, but Jim kept at it. The primary period his work was intended to cover was from 1870, when a weekly edition of the *Tucson Citizen* began being published, to February 1912, when Arizona achieved statehood. Jim quickly realized, however, that in reviewing issues of the *Citizen* and *Arizona Daily Star* he would be looking mostly at articles that had nothing to do with the Chinese. So, Jim decided to broaden the scope of his work, and it started getting more extensive—much more extensive. Eventually, his handwritten notes comprised almost three hundred subject categories. Organizational and funding support from the Tucson Corral of the Westerners, complemented by grants generously supplied by the Southwestern Foundation for Education and Historical Preservation along with the Tucson-Pima County Historical Commission, were provided. Mary Ellen Thompson was then hired in 2005 to input this growing body of material into electronic spreadsheets.

Jim Ayres was diagnosed with leukemia during this project, but he kept working, intent on completing it. He did so before his 2015 death. Mary Ellen Thompson and I then undertook the challenge of organizing the remaining draft material. That process took some time, but when finished, the Jim

Ayres Newspaper Index was presented in both hard copy and electronic format to the Arizona Historical Society Library; it is now also on the AHS website. The index was also provided to the Special Collections Library at the University of Arizona and the Pima County Public Library. While many of the listings are briefly annotated, for those without annotations, Arizona Pathfinders Inc. has kindly contributed ongoing financial support to help fill in many of these blanks.

The work that Jim Ayres did on his newspaper index is the foundation for this review of territorial Tucson. Without it, this book simply wouldn't have been possible.

Several other people deserve recognition. Rachael Black and the other librarians at the Arizona Historical Society in Tucson were extremely helpful. Their friendliness and support with the ongoing effort to review and copy hundreds of newspaper stories are greatly appreciated.

Also helpful was acquisitions editor Lindsey Givens of The History Press, with whom I worked throughout the process. Her comments on the draft text, review of the submitted images and overall assistance with the project were very helpful.

Alice Bowman deserves special praise for both her analysis of the images I proposed to include along with her editorial suggestions. Not only did she coordinate the compilation of the images used, but Alice also made cogent comments about the draft text. For that and all the other assistance she provided, I am profoundly grateful.

Finally, the help my wife, Susie Morris, gave me by locating newspaper stories on numerous rolls of microfilm, copying the articles and then commenting on their potential usefulness was tremendous. Her assistance reduced the research time for this project to a reasonable period, and I am sincerely appreciative.

The final phases of the publication process were completed during the 2020 COVID-19 pandemic. Everyone involved with the book's preparation pulled together to successfully complete the project.

This book is based on several sources of information, not just newspaper stories. Sometimes those sources conflict, and I've tried my best to determine the accuracy of the material. If I have failed in some cases and made mistakes, I take full responsibility.

This book is a project that involved several people and many months to complete. It was the work of Jim Ayres in compiling his index of early southern Arizona English-language newspapers, however, that inspired me to write it. That is why I have dedicated this book to him.

INTRODUCTION

Scattered across a tabletop, jigsaw pieces are curiously shaped individual entities. As they are combined, however, an image slowly emerges until the whole picture can be comprehended. The same might be said about perspectives of history. As a series of events occurring at a single point in time or in a continuum are considered, themes or trends may be understood. Thus, a knowledge of history can, hopefully, be used as a predictor of future occurrences.

This history of territorial Tucson includes a number of topics, from snake stories to transportation methods to residential development. By contemplating these subjects individually, the reader will have a better understanding about just how diverse Tucson was before statehood. It might not have been a large place, but it certainly had a lot going on in many respects.

One of those was racial and gender differences. The role that slavery played in bringing southern Arizona into the United States, and then the ardent support it had among Tucson's earliest European American residents, was a harbinger of other ethnic positions. These men's racial antagonisms had been clearly demonstrated before the Civil War toward Native Americans and would later be shown toward most Mexican Americans, as well as the Chinese residents of town. At the same time, many women, though not all, were relegated to "stay at home" roles.

From the time of their arrival in the 1850s, European American men were the dominant force in local business and politics. That was partially due to their access to capital. It was additionally a result of their limiting voting rights mostly to themselves. That monopoly on political and economic power was rarely breached. Sometimes, however, because of their economic achievements, men like Estevan Ochoa and women like Annie Box Neal were partially spared all the realities of discrimination.

That is a legacy that Tucson residents don't often consider, but it is part of our history. Telling at least a few of these stories was a goal of this book. But history is certainly not all dark skies and frowns. Relaying some lighthearted instances about celebrations, sports and individual personalities was another objective of the book. Combined, all of these portraits will hopefully make a clearer picture of what territorial Tucson was actually like.

At the same time, some important subjects get little or no attention because they have been extensively covered elsewhere. Politics, criminal activity, early aviation, the growth of the University of Arizona and public education are generally not reviewed.

What is included throughout the book is the cost of goods and services at the time of citation. To compare these prices to today's values, a multiplier of approximately thirty can be used to provide a rough estimate of current value. For example, the cost of voting in 1906 (due to a poll tax) was $2.50; in 2020, that amount would be about $72.00.

Another frequently used word is *Papago*, for referring to the native people who have lived in the Tucson region for centuries. While the correct current term is *Tohono O'odham*, since *Papago* was the word used during territorial times, it is what is found in the text.

A general knowledge of territorial Tucson can give us clues about why the community's later history had some of the characteristics it did. Before statehood, Tucson was a diverse but racially divided place. That didn't change for decades and is still being debated today.

Additionally, women by the 1890s began playing a more important role in Tucson, and their influence only grew after that. Once they achieved voting rights in 1913, their political importance became even greater, but it would be more than a century before a woman was elected mayor of Tucson.

The community's leaders in territorial times also had ambitions to retain Tucson's distinction as the major metropolitan area in Arizona and took steps to ensure that happened. Improvement projects, sometimes with governmental financial backing, were frequently proposed but often did not come to fruition for various reasons. Despite that, grandiose development plans and schemes kept getting proposed. That is a characteristic the community has continued into the twenty-first century.

All of these stories, from delightful to distasteful, help make up the jigsaw puzzle of Tucson before statehood. Knowledge of them can perhaps provide us with a little understanding of why things today, at least in some cases, are the way they are. They can also assist us to see how positive change came about, often extremely slowly. Hopefully this book will help tell some of these stories successfully by illuminating at least a part of the puzzle of territorial Tucson.

Chapter 1

FROM PURCHASE TO TERRITORY

Quiteria Munguía accomplished something truly extraordinary in 1860 Tucson when the U.S. Census listed her as being one hundred years old. During the century of Quiteria's life, the tiny community of Tucson had gone through several major changes. Established as a Spanish military outpost in 1775, the extremely isolated settlement became part of Mexico when that country gained its independence in 1821. Then, in 1854, the Gadsden Purchase brought Tucson into the United States. She didn't know it then, but Quiteria and other residents were shifting countries because in far-off Washington, D.C., some politicians were dreaming of a southern coast-to-coast railroad.

During the 1840s, calls to extend the nation from ocean to ocean intensified, in part because of the desire to build a transcontinental railroad to facilitate trade with China. Much of the land west of the existing border, set by the United States 1845 annexation of Texas, was still Mexican territory. Thus, the prospects for a transcontinental railroad on exclusively American soil looked dim. Despite that, among those calling for a southern pathway to the Pacific Ocean was James Gadsden, a railway executive and plantation slave owner from South Carolina.

After the 1846 start of the Mexican-American War, J.D.B. DeBow, editor of the *Commercial Review* journal in New Orleans and another supporter of a southern transcontinental route, suggested that the "right-of-way for a railroad through such region of Mexico to the Pacific…should by all means be exacted." Then he added forthrightly, "Let us demand the right-of-way from Mexico."

James Gadsden, negotiator of the 1854 Gadsden Purchase. *National Archives, photo no. 111-SC-88521.*

In preparing an initial proposed peace treaty to end the hostilities with Mexico, poorly informed officials of the State Department in Washington, D.C., established the Gila River, well north of Tucson, as part of the proposed new boundary line. With the eastern stretches of that river running through extremely mountainous terrain, the problems with that decision for railroad building were soon pointed out to Secretary of State James Buchanan by First Lieutenant William H. Emory. On their way to California, Emory had led a surveying crew across the imposing upper Gila River region in 1846 and concluded that it was not conducive to track-laying. Emory thought that the area farther south, though, would make ideal territory for railroad construction. "It is possible to pass through the mountain system in this region," he wrote, "near the parallel of 32° [of latitude], almost on the level of the plateau." Despite that informed opinion, the 1848 Treaty of Guadalupe Hidalgo ending the war with Mexico used the Gila River as part of the new border. For $15 million, the treaty also transferred an enormous amount of property to the United States that would allow for a central transcontinental railroad route to be built entirely across American land.

Many southerners, including U.S. Senator Jefferson Davis from Mississippi, were understandably outraged by that outcome. Hoping to export slavery westward, Davis wrote of a possible southern transcontinental route:

> *If we had a good railroad and other roads making it convenient to go through Texas into New Mexico, and through New Mexico into southern California, our people with their servants, their horses and their cows would gradually pass westward over fertile lands into mining districts, and in the latter, especially, the advantage of their associated labor* [slaves] *would impress itself upon others about them and the prejudice which now shuts us out of that country would yield to the persuasion of personal interest.*

When Davis was appointed secretary of war in 1853 by newly elected president Franklin Pierce, he suggested that James Gadsden be named ambassador to Mexico. His primary task would be to obtain more land in order to accommodate a southern railway across U.S. territory. After short but intense negotiations, a draft treaty was finalized in Mexico City at the end of 1853, but during the Senate's spring 1854 ratification process, almost everything in Gadsden's draft proposal was substantially altered. The final approved treaty—known as the Gadsden Purchase but which Gadsden himself disavowed because of the Senate's drastically revised boundary line and the treaty's onerous conditions placed on Mexico—paid that nation $10 million for almost thirty thousand square miles of land. This territory south of the Gila River would allow a transcontinental railroad, known as the 32° route, to eventually be built. According to the *Enquirer* newspaper in Richmond, Virginia, the treaty would also give "the South a chance for two or three more slave States."

The new U.S. land at first would become part of the existing territory of New Mexico, which stretched all the way from Texas to California. Additionally, the purchase would bring Tucson, a small settlement on the banks of the often intermittent Santa Cruz River, into the United States and send a few U.S. soldiers briefly to the community in 1856. "I have often heard my mother say," Tucsonan Carmen Lucero recalled in a 1928 interview, "that the coming of the Americans…was a God send to Tucson for the [Apache] Indians had killed off many of the Mexicans and the poor were being ground down by the rich. The day the troops took possession there was lots of excitement. They raised the flag on the wall and the people welcomed them with a fiesta and they were all on good terms."

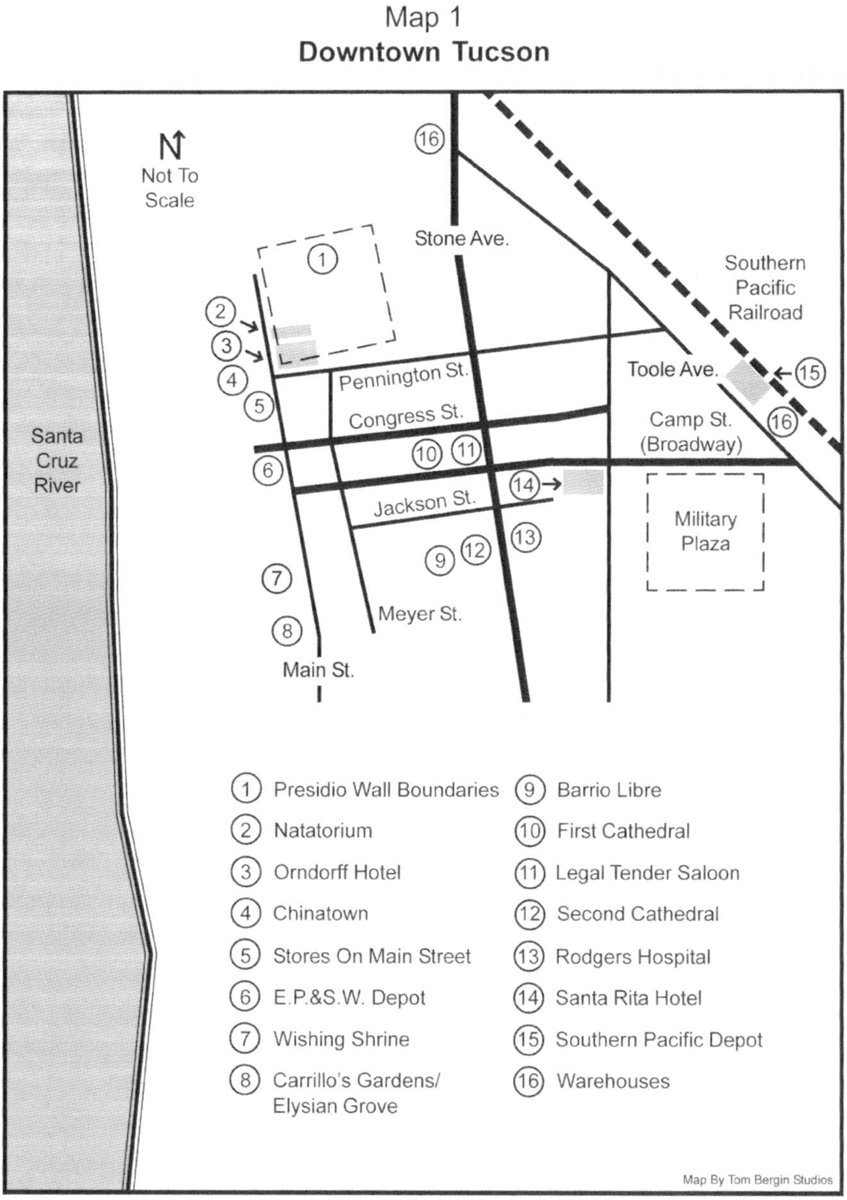

Downtown Tucson in territorial times. *Map by Tom Bergin, 2020.*

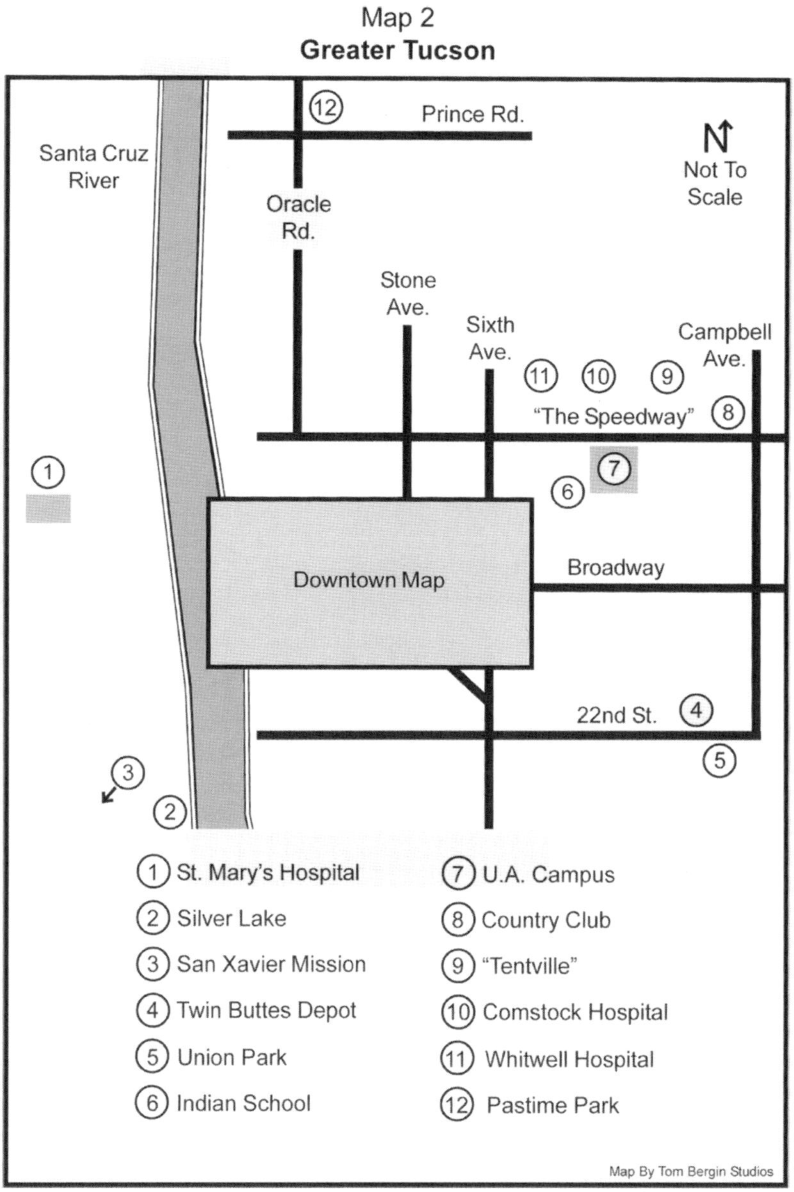

Greater Tucson in territorial times. *Map by Tom Bergin, 2020.*

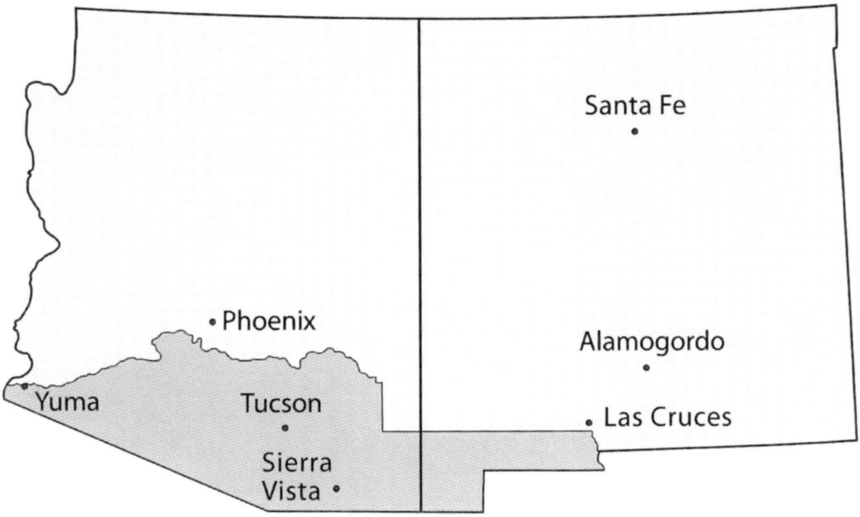

The 1854 Gadsden Purchase shown in the eventual U.S. territories of Arizona and New Mexico. *Wikimedia Commons*.

That reaction wasn't surprising. While the area had been the site of permanent human habitation for about four thousand years, before the Gadsden Purchase only about five hundred Mexicans were living in isolated Tucson within the adobe (sun-dried mud brick) walls of a fort, or presidio. It had been built by Spanish troops in the 1770s as protection against Apache raids, even as some of the region's Papagos and other native peoples lived in harmony with the newcomers. Along with their soldier husbands, many women resided in the nearly thirteen-acre presidio. "Women cared for their households, raised children, and tended to gardens," summarized historical archaeologist J. Homer Thiel. While Mexican mule trains from the south imported a few items—including rice, fabrics and chocolate—Thiel reported of Tucson: "Settlers relied on locally made goods, such as Native American pottery, to meet many of their needs."

Arizona was described around that time as "dry, sterile, hilly country—scarcely fit for anything else than stock raising and mining." While many things in Tucson remained the same in the years immediately following the Gadsden Purchase, others changed. One was the issue of slavery. It had been banned by Mexico in 1829 but still was possible in the territories of the United States.

Another thing that changed was the physical shape of the community. The presidio's walls slowly came down because of deterioration and vandalism, and the small town began incrementally expanding to the south and west because the population was increasing slightly. As author Neil B. Carmony summarized of Tucson at that time: "The village itself consisted of a collection of unimposing one-story adobe buildings scattered along dusty dirt streets. Tucson very much resembled a rural Mexican pueblo."

By 1860, there were approximately 625 residents of Tucson. Of these, about 440 had been born in either Mexico or New Mexico and were almost evenly split between males and females. Only 13 of the 140 people born elsewhere in the Americas, however, were women. Just 7 people in Tucson were also listed by the census as either being Black or mulatto, with 5 of them belonging to the Isiah Bell family. At this time, 4 U.S. soldiers were in town, and there were also 41 people from other nations, including 10 from Ireland.

"Life was very simple," Carmen Lucero remarked of those times. "Each man had his little piece of land [along the Santa Cruz River] down below the walled city where he raised beans, lentils, onions, squash, *garvanzas* [garbanzos], chili, wheat, tomatoes, and corn. There were some fruit trees with peaches, pears, and quinces. Most everybody raised pigs, rendered lard, and made salt pork."

Tucson's presidio chapel "On San Antonio's Day (June 13), 1860." *From* The Loyal West in the Times of the Rebellion *by John W. Barber.*

The outsiders who had arrived in Tucson after the Gadsden Purchase were not impressed by what they found. "Early Anglo visitors to Tucson considered the pueblo primitive and backward," concluded historian Thomas Sheridan in *Los Tucsonenses: The Mexican Community in Tucson, 1854–1941*. But as he rightfully pointed out of the existing residents, "the simple fact was that Tucsonenses had learned over the years to live with scarcity and isolation. Theirs was a rough and dangerous life."

The arriving newcomers, mostly men from eastern states or Europe, had to learn Spanish out of necessity. Because some of them had access to investment income for mining, ranching and other commercial ventures, they quickly became the dominant economic force in town. "In a sense," Sheridan wrote, "Tucson in 1860 was a dual, almost schizophrenic, settlement, one divided between Mexican families rooted in the land and aggressive young male Anglo immigrants seeking fame and fortune on the Apache frontier."

Many of these wealth-seeking young men quickly sided with the Confederacy after the early March 1861 inauguration of President Abraham Lincoln. One of those advocating that rebellious choice was Granville H. Oury, an attorney who had come to Arizona in 1856 at thirty-one years of age. At a late March 1861 Tucson meeting held "for the purpose of giving expression to the feelings and sentiments of the community, as to whether they would seek protection from a Northern or a Southern Confederacy," Oury was one of five European American men appointed to a committee to draft a resolution of support. When they reported back two days later, they blamed the pending military conflict on northern aggression and hostility "upon the cherished institutions of the South." The committee proposed that all those Tucson men allowed to vote on the measure should endorse "that under any and all circumstances our sympathies are with the Southern Confederacy." This resolution was then adopted by a substantial majority.

After Civil War fighting began, the only Federal troops in the region—the one hundred or so stationed well south of Tucson at Fort Buchanan close to the Mexican border—were sent eastward in July 1861. According to one Tucson commentator, loss of these troops meant that "the [Apache] Indians will have it all their own way."

In response to this Union move, by August 1861, Southern officials had declared the region south of 34° latitude, formerly part of the New Mexico Territory, to be called Arizona and to be controlled by a Confederate military government. In apparent compliance, a Rebel flag in September 1861 was raised above the former presidio. The *Nevada Democrat*, a California

A Confederate battle flag. *From istockphoto.com.*

newspaper, stated of the flag in Tucson: "[It] shows that her citizens acknowledge no allegiance to abolition rule."

Around the same time, while not everyone in town favored the South and boycotted his selection, Oury was unanimously chosen as a delegate to the Congress of the Confederate States of America by sixty-eight European American men still residing in Tucson. Seeking military protection from Apache raids, Oury and many of the others also wanted the region south of the 34° to become an official Confederate territory. It had been less than ten years since Jefferson Davis and James Gadsden had supported exporting slavery to California, and their hope was apparently moving toward realization when on November 25, 1861, a bill to establish the Territory of Arizona was introduced in the Congress of the Confederate States of America meeting at Richmond, Virginia. Oury traveled to Richmond to take up his delegate position and speak on the proposal, which stipulated that "the institution of slavery in said [Arizona] Territory shall receive all necessary protection, both from the Territorial legislature and the Congress of the Confederate States." Oury also wrote of the proposed territory "that the people of Arizona [are] loyal and devoted to the South."

That loyalty was soon rewarded when the bill establishing the Arizona Territory passed on January 13, 1862. Confederate president Jefferson Davis made it official one month later when he signed the legislation making Arizona a Rebel territory, with a northern boundary line at the 34° latitude and the capital at Mesilla, far to the east of remote Tucson.

Also in early 1862, Confederate troops from Texas were ordered to take possession of Tucson in order to protect "the important and growing interest, chiefly mineral, in Western Arizona and for the further purpose of opening communications with Southern California." These troops numbered about one hundred, and they occupied unprotected Tucson by the end of February. Their arrival "was hailed by a majority [of the population]" according to one source, but some locals, including businessman Estevan Ochoa, ardently pledged their support for the Union and voluntarily left town.

After a large contingent of the California Column of Union troops arrived in Arizona in May 1862, and a small patrol of them skirmished

Mississippi senator Jefferson Davis, future president of the Confederate States of America. *Library of Congress, photo no. 26716.*

with some Rebels at Picacho north of Tucson, the Southerners eventually skedaddled back to Texas. Oury went with them to serve as an officer in the Confederate army and would unsuccessfully lobby as late as 1864 for another invasion of Arizona by Rebel forces. While Oury had gone east, many other Tucson supporters of the Confederacy fled to Mexico. The small community of Tucson, labeled a "nest hole of traitors" by one Northerner, was then easily secured by Union soldiers. "The citizens of the town came out and met the [approaching Union] troops in great numbers," reported the *San Francisco Evening Bulletin* newspaper of the happenings in Arizona, "greeting them with cheers."

Several months later, the U.S. Congress in Washington, D.C. continued its long-running discussion about whether to make Arizona a Union territory separate from New Mexico. While Congress had earlier allowed the legislature of the New Mexico Territory to decide whether slavery would be permitted, in Rebel-supporting Arizona that choice wasn't going to be offered. Instead, for Confederate-leaning Tucson and the surrounding region, the draft enabling act creating the territory specifically prohibited slavery.

When the U.S. Senate, on February 20, 1863, debated the issue of Arizona becoming a Union territory, the mineral wealth of the region was certainly relished. "It is thought to be as rich in gold and silver, and especially the latter, as any part of the earth" Senator Benjamin F. Wade of Ohio noted. "It would be very well to have a little gold and silver to mix up with our greenbacks," he quipped.

Some senators wanted to amend the draft legislation to allow territorial residents to determine their position on slavery; the majority of senators, however, voted to include in the territorial act language outright banning slavery. The revised legislation was finally approved by a Senate vote of twenty-five to twelve, and President Lincoln signed it on February 24. A few weeks later, the *Evening Star* newspaper in the nation's capital reported of Arizona, "Our California advisers inform us that already in anticipation of military protection, large bodies of miners are flocking towards this new El Dorado."

Arizona was a U.S. territory less than a decade after the Gadsden Purchase, and Tucson was its largest settlement. The 1864 census found more than 1,050 people in town, and at least 650 of them were listed as either being born locally or nearby. Another 300 residents said they originally came from Mexico. While the number of Mexican Americans and Mexican nationals in Tucson had grown substantially since 1860, those from elsewhere in the United States showed a significant drop from four years earlier. Their numbers had fallen from 140 to only 69, presumably because of the departure of Southern supporters.

Also in 1864, there were 250 U.S. troops stationed in Tucson. After retaking the town, the Union soldiers initially established a camp near the Santa Cruz River. For some time after that, soldiers would come and go, but on July 29, 1866, the 70 men of Company C of the First Cavalry arrived and within a month established a permanent post to be called Camp Lowell. It was located on a large vacant area about half a mile southeast of the former presidio. The ongoing presence of the U.S. Army, however, wouldn't sway the fond feelings toward the Confederacy of many of the remaining European Americans in Tucson. More than three months after Robert E. Lee had surrendered at Appomattox in April 1865, it was still said of the community, "[N]early all the people there are of the [secession] persuasion."

Chapter 2

SNAKE STORIES

What could six seemingly unrelated things—injecting ammonia, common baking soda, desert plant extract, bottled solution, sliced onion and smoking cigars—possibly have had in common in territorial Tucson? Each was once proclaimed a cure for venomous snakebites.

The remedy of injecting ammonia into a bite wound appeared in an 1876 edition of the *Arizona Citizen* newspaper. It referenced a Melbourne, Australia publication that cited four cases of an almost instantaneous "magical effect." Two years later, baking soda applied on a rattlesnake wound was announced to be another certain cure.

For bite victims who didn't have baking soda lying around, a supposed traditional Papago technique was suggested in 1894 by a miner named Hutchinson. After chewing a plant identified as snakeweed, the poultice created would be applied to the wound. "The natives of the country who are familiar with its uses," the *Citizen* pointed out, "make no claim to its infallibility as an antidote."

The next year, a "Snake King" salesman was in Tucson trying to peddle snake oil of questionable value. Unlike the native people of southern Arizona, the "King" wasn't reluctant to guarantee his product. After supposedly allowing himself to be bitten by two rattlesnakes, he showed how the oil could do "wonderful things."

The idea of paying a high price to purchase a snakebite product of dubious reliability was just malarkey according to miner Charles Lovett.

A rattlesnake. *Photo by Tim Vickers, 2008, Wikimedia Commons.*

He claimed to have been bitten numerous times, and in 1897, a black diamondback rattler got him in the Dragoon Mountains southeast of Tucson. Charles wasn't fazed, the *Citizen* explained, because he didn't mind "a snake bite [any] more than an attack by a mosquito. He knows of a simple remedy which is most always close at hand and beats any snake poison antidote extract. He applies the fresh cut side of half an onion to the wound, and while waiting boils two or three of the same and applies them. Relief follows quickly."

That dubious solution, like the others, was listed infrequently in local papers. But another remedy for snakebites was mentioned across many years. In his store, merchant Sam Drachman sold Key West cigars and proudly and repeatedly advertised that smoking one would render harmless "the bite of a rattlesnake, sting of a bee, or inflammation from a rusty nail."

While obviously offered as comic relief, Drachman's antidote did mention a sometimes serious issue. Even though rattlesnake bites apparently weren't all that common around Tucson during territorial times, they could have fatal consequences. In May 1880, former U.S. Army private Samuel C. Whipple one night went out in his bare feet to close his corral gate. He unluckily stepped on a rattlesnake that bit him. Whipple tried the ammonia remedy, but it didn't work. Within two days, he had died after "the most intense suffering and pain."

Another fatality south of Tucson was narrowly avoided in 1911 when a rattlesnake struck railroad worker Gus Holstrom on the arm. By the time he reached town seeking medical treatment, Holstrom's condition was listed as "his arm was swollen to almost four times its normal size and when he entered the hospital, it is stated, his case was considered desperate." Thankfully, he apparently survived.

Also escaping with his life was miner J.O. Johnson, but he did have a terrifying experience that, he thought, "would turn a man's hair white." It must have been a cool October 1907 evening, as Johnson recalled, because while he slept a rattlesnake more than seven feet in length that was seeking warmth crawled into bed with him. Startled and afraid to move or make a sound to ask for help from his tent mate, Johnson lay as still as possible. Finally, his companion awoke and suggested Johnson cut a hole in the tent and jump through it. Miraculously, he did it successfully!

It wasn't only possible cures and actual and avoided snakebites that territorial Tucson newspaper readers learned about. In 1892, druggist Fred Fleishman had both a bull and rattlesnake on public display in the front window of his west Congress Street shop. Fifteen years later, another druggist, George Martin, did the same thing in his store, but this time with "a bunch of rattlers and other deadly snakes."

George Martin (*left*) in his 1890 pharmacy. He would later use snakes to promote the business. *University of Arizona College of Pharmacy Museum.*

That exhibit was just child's play compared to something that happened in 1907. A traveling tent show had set up on Congress Street and charged ten cents to see its star attraction, the "Australian Wild Girl." But during her performance with a poisonous moccasin snake, the reptile bit her on the tongue as some in the crowd screamed in horror. It was said of the victim that her face grew grotesquely swollen and her tongue black and huge. Doctors were called, and they applied antidotes while making a totally unexpected discovery. The "Wild Girl" turned out to be John Pike, a performer dressed in a deceptive costume who was described as a "fairly good looking young man." While the tent show moved along the next day, Pike remained in town to recover.

That was only one of dozens of stories about snakes appearing in territorial Tucson newspapers. Among the first was an 1871 article that explained how the water snakes at the Nine Mile Water Hole northwest of town were terribly emaciated because the frogs they ate had dropped in number due to disease.

Despite that problem, as early as 1875 the Smithsonian Institution in Washington, D.C., was expressing interest in acquiring southern Arizona snakes. In a letter to brewer, storekeeper and early schoolteacher John Spring, in exchange for "suitable compensation" to him, a representative of the Smithsonian asked him to "gather whatever you can in the way of small snakes, lizards, etc." and send them to the nation's capital.

While lizards were abundant in the area, that request may not have been all that easy to fulfill for venomous snakes. As one commentator observed in 1880 of rattlesnakes, "I have seen but few of them during my sojourn in the territory." When the summer monsoon rains came in 1887, however, the *Citizen* noted that "rattlers are said to be quite plentiful on the mesas bordering on the Rillito [Creek]."

An attempt to turn collecting snakes into a profitable business failed in 1909. The Arizona Snake Company was established in Tucson "to secure for shipment rattlesnakes, Gila monsters, scorpions, tarantulas, centipedes, and other reptiles." Up to eighteen dollars would be paid for one dozen, good-sized, live rattlesnakes, and they, and the other creatures, would be shipped to New York City on their way to Europe. From the information available, the business didn't last long.

When they were seen, however, local snakes sometimes were described with extraordinary characteristics. A miner working near Calabasas south of town in 1880 encountered "a snake with red and white stripes running around its body, that was 24 feet long." Perhaps the man got the snake confused with a huge, rolled up American flag?

Another reported use for rattlesnakes was as an alarm clock. The *Citizen* in 1895 stated that two miners shot a rattlesnake that had come "within striking distance" of one of the men while he was in bed. The *Weekly Star* turned that true story into an extremely tall tale. "The snake is trained to approach the head of the bed," the newspaper wrote in jest, "and sound his tocsin [warning signal]. He may not be as regular as an alarm clock, but the main advantage about the system is that when a man is awakened that way, he doesn't roll over on the other side and fall into a doze....He is 'up for all day.'"

People would obviously pay rapt attention to that fictional method of awakening, but occasionally snakes were attributed with little-known traits they might actually possess. In 1895, merchant, rancher and former Pima County treasurer Thomas Hughes had a fig crop that kept disappearing. He accused his sons of theft and consumption, but they pleaded innocence. Instead, they were able to show their father two diamondback rattlesnakes improbably in the tree, one of which had a fig in its mouth.

It wasn't climbing snakes but huge serpents that sometimes gathered public attention in Tucson. In 1892, the Spanish-language newspaper *El Fronterizo* reported on a forty-foot-long deceased British specimen that might have been 1 million years old. Could this have been, the story asked, the biblical serpent that tempted Eve? Then in 1894, a two-hundred-foot-long sea serpent was claimed to be off Vera Cruz, Mexico. "[T]he monster had a very small head," the *Weekly Star* stated, "which it carried out of the water in an upright position to a height of 15 feet."

That incredible, and hard-to-believe, story had nothing on one printed in August 1891. The entire nation was going through economically rough times, and Tucson was no exception. The city's population had fallen by more than 25 percent from 7,000 in 1880 to 5,150 a decade later. Construction had stopped almost completely, and many people were severely depressed about the community's prospects. To counter that pessimism, the *Citizen* ran a long story that was headlined, "Sea Serpent—Seven Headed Monster Below Town—Came Up the Santa Cruz—He Is Viewed by Frightened Hundreds from Town—Delivers a Homily and Prophesy—Comes from Salton."

Apparently, a man passing through town relayed to local folks how he had just encountered a huge sea serpent in the Santa Cruz River. People laughed at the idea until they followed the man down to the water's edge, which was swollen by summer monsoon rains. In the light of a full moon, the amazed crowd reportedly saw a seven-headed, four-hundred-foot-long serpent that helpfully spoke perfect English. The incredible creature told

Unlike this sea serpent, Tucson's 1891 giant watery visitor had seven heads and spoke perfect English. *From istockphoto.com.*

those people who had not fainted from fright that he came from the three-hundred-square-mile Salton Sea in Southern California and had journeyed to Tucson to convey a prophecy about its future.

Taking a seat on the riverside watermelon patch of a Chinese farmer, among many things the enormous serpent sermonized:

> *The rainfall of Arizona shall be increased fourfold thereby, and the land shall rejoice and be glad, more especially in this fine valley on which I have smiled and poured forth my bounty.…Behold this valley on which the bounty of all earth shall appear. It shall grow and be fruitful in abundance.… Men will come more and more, their homes shall be many where now the beasts of the field wander in peace undisturbed. Yea, this valley shall be a mighty and happy one. Houses shall become mansions, the poor shall enrichen, the desert shall be filled.*

With that, the imposing creature dove into the rushing river water and disappeared. According to the *Citizen*, the serpent's promise of a fruitful future for Tucson was one those who heard it truly believed.

Chapter 3

LOCOMOTIVES, BICYCLES AND LOCOMOBILES

It wasn't giant sea serpents that Tucson residents years earlier had believed would bring them economic prosperity. Many people in town instead were looking forward to the promised financial bonanza that a southern cross-country rail line could mean. Steel rails would certainly increase the exploitation of the rich mineral wealth of the region. In addition, according to territorial governor Richard McCormick in 1868, the easier access for more troops a railroad could provide would be "one of the most important steps toward the subjugation of the Apache that can be taken."

If that new transcontinental line passed through Tucson, the *Weekly Arizonian* newspaper speculated in 1871, the community could become a railroad hub, with other tracks soon running to Guaymas, Sonora, Mexico. Following passage that same year of a bill giving the Texas Pacific Railroad Company the Congressional authorization needed to build a transcontinental line across Texas to El Paso and then westward to San Diego, that possibility seemed achievable.

The company, however, wanted substantial federal government subsidies, and when it didn't receive them, it failed to lay much track in Texas. Thus, by 1875, the four men who owned the western half of the first transcontinental line—Charles Crocker, Mark Hopkins, Collis Huntington and Leland Stanford—had purchased the Southern Pacific Company of California, intent on building the second cross-country railroad. They wanted to lay tracks from Los Angeles to New Orleans and planned to finance the project themselves.

To permit this work, the Arizona legislature in 1877 adopted a bill allowing Southern Pacific to cross the territory. Introduced by Tucson freight company owner Estevan Ochoa, the act would mean competition from the railroad for his horse-drawn wagon business, but he sponsored it anyway.

Three years later, at the Toole Avenue depot site on March 20, 1880, Crocker stepped off the first ceremonial passenger train to arrive in Tucson. It was fitting that Ochoa was chosen to present him with a silver spike to memorialize an occasion that the *Citizen* labeled "the greatest event in the history of this city." The coming of the railroad would mean many things. Slow passenger travel by stagecoach and freighting by wagon train would be replaced by faster movement by rails. Lumber for construction would be more easily available at lower prices, as would modern fashions and furnishings.

New varieties of fruits and vegetables would also result because Chinese men had begun arriving in Tucson around 1875. There were only a few of them until the Southern Pacific track work (done primarily by Chinese laborers) halted for the summer of 1879 at Casa Grande, sixty miles north of town. Some of the laid-off laborers decided to settle in Tucson, where they took up various occupations, including farming. When they did, the *Star*, whose editor and publisher was Louis C. Hughes, stated unapologetically that the Chinese were "an ignorant, filthy, leperous horde of beings who may have the form of a human being but lack every element which enters into true American civilization." The *Citizen* took the opposite perspective, pointing out that in fields along the Santa Cruz River, Chinese farmers would grow crops different from their Mexican American competitors. "Just think of it," the newspaper predicted joyously in 1880, "'strawberries and cream' in Tucson next year."

One important product the railroad wouldn't introduce to the desert town, at least directly, was ice. In the blistering hot summer of 1879, the first delivery of it came by stage from Casa Grande. The cold commodity was delivered to Schultz's soda fountain, and the *Star* exclaimed excitedly of the chilly treasure, "Our people may expect to be treated daily to ice cold drink." Within a few months, ice was being manufactured in Tucson, and by the end of 1879, two ice plants were in business.

Not only had 1880 seen the arrival of the railroad, but it was also the year former Confederate politician and soldier Granville Oury was elected as the Arizona Territory's delegate to the U.S. Congress. After the end of Civil War hostilities, Oury took an oath of allegiance to the Union in October 1865. Less than twelve months later, he was elected from Pima County to the territorial legislature and then was appointed Arizona's attorney general in 1869. He moved to Phoenix in 1871 and later to Florence, Arizona, from

Tucson's first Southern Pacific Railroad depot opened in 1880 on Toole Avenue. *Arizona Historical Society, Buehman #BN 137.*

where he was elected twice to Congress. Despite Oury's departure from Tucson, the former supporter of slavery still had many friends in southern Arizona. When he received the 1880 nomination of the Democratic Party to Congress, the *Citizen*, a strongly Republican newspaper, wrote glowingly of him, "No man in the Territory has a better record than Mr. Oury." In Washington, D.C., Oury would be one of only sixteen men ever to serve in the Confederate Congress who later became a member of the U.S. Congress.

Black residents of the region, about seventy-five of whom were in Tucson in 1880, weren't lauded like Oury. The *Star*, in an article from the previous year, had praised the Sixth Cavalry residing at Fort Lowell eight miles east of town, where the troops had moved from the center of Tucson several years earlier. The newspaper then derogatorily added of the African Americans in the Ninth Cavalry stationed in New Mexico, "We now express a hope that these negro soldiers will never be brought into Arizona—we desire our lives and property to be protected by white men."

Concerning railroads, the 1880 arrival of Southern Pacific trains meant that the first step had been taken in the planned transition of Tucson into a rail hub. Within two years, the proposal was made to build a line to Port Lobos on Mexico's Gulf of California. While the *Citizen* acknowledged that Port Lobos was neither a port nor a town, it thought the barren property perfect for development. "Its location and the excellence of the harbor," the newspaper stated in July 1882, "are sufficiently [*sic*] to indicate the prediction that it will some day be a metropolitan port."

Nothing was implemented on that railroad project, but across the decades the idea kept popping up. By 1909, twenty-seven years after the concept was originally floated, the *Star* stated, "[T]he Port Lobos [rail]road will positively be constructed and that Tucson will be its eastern terminal." But it never happened.

In 1885, two other Tucson railroad possibilities arose. Both a line south to the Calabasas mining region near the Mexican border as well as laying narrow-gauge tracks northward to the copper town of Globe were proposed. Work actually began on the narrow-gauge line in July 1885, and about nine miles of track were laid, including a bridge across the Rillito Creek north of town. But despite financial backing from the Pima County government, work on the line stopped due to monetary difficulties. Scuttlebutt spread in 1887 that track-laying was to resume, but a monsoon storm in September of that year washed out the bridge. The narrow-gauge railroad, despite more years of rumors to the contrary, was no more.

Even though a railroad line south from Tucson had been contemplated since 1885, it wasn't until the twentieth century that talk of laying tracks eighteen miles to the Twin Buttes mining district finally turned into reality. By January 1906, a tiny, 512-square-foot depot for the Twin Buttes railroad had been completed at First Avenue and Twenty-Second Street in Tucson, and track-laying was about

Workers at the Twin Buttes mine, circa 1905. The mine's railroad opened with a celebration on July 4, 1906. *From* Ghost Towns of Arizona *(1968), Wikimedia Commons.*

to commence with 160 men. The copper mine the line would serve employed about 100 laborers working three shifts, and it was owned by David S. Rose, the longtime mayor of Milwaukee, Wisconsin. He visited southern Arizona frequently and said that he enjoyed his time in the "sun-kiss" land. The route was finished on the Fourth of July 1906, and a grand celebration was held at the mining camp. The initial timetable showed one train per day leaving Twin Buttes at 6:45 a.m. and taking until 8:30 a.m. to reach Tucson. The return trip commenced at 12:40 p.m., with three possible stops along the way back.

Following completion of the Twin Buttes line, implementation of the Tucson and West Coast of Mexico Railroad eventually happened. Ten miles of track had been laid northward between Nogales, Arizona, and Calabasas in 1882, and the new Twin Buttes line ran to Sahuarita south of Tucson. In 1910, a Southern Pacific associated company purchased the Twin Buttes Railroad and put in thirty-eight miles of track to connect Sahuarita with Calabasas. Finally, Tucson was directly connected to the rail lines of Mexico, and the one-way fare from town to Nogales, Arizona, was $3.45. At the same time, the Twenty-Second Street depot of the Twin Buttes Railroad was closed, with operations moved to the Southern Pacific train station on Toole Avenue.

To mark the 1910 opening of the Tucson and West Coast of Mexico Railroad line, the presidents of Mexico and the United States—Porfirio Díaz and William H. Taft, respectively—were invited to attend a local ceremony. Both, of course, sent telegrams of congratulations instead. Taft's applauded the strengthening of "the bonds of friendship already existing between the peoples of the two countries." For its part, the *Citizen* was exuberant in its praise for the community and its prospects: "Tucson is already one of the important commercial and social centers of the Southwest and the city is in its infancy."

Anticipation of even more regional economic gain due to railroad development had been strengthened in 1907 when talk surfaced of implementing another transcontinental line that could pass through Tucson. The proposed route would combine a San Diego to Yuma, Arizona pathway with the extension of the existing El Paso and Southwestern Railroad (EP&SW) from Fairbank, Arizona, into Tucson and then on to Yuma. The tracks in California of the severely topographically challenged line labeled the "Impossible Railroad," however, never made it close to the Colorado River and Yuma.

The Phelps Dodge Corporation, owner of the EP&SW, on the other hand, was serious about its expansion plans. Believing that the mining company's route could possibly bypass Tucson and head to Phoenix instead, local leaders put together a $75,000 package of financial inducements to ensure that the line came to town. To raise the subsidy money, which in the words of supporters was needed to guarantee "Tucson be made the great railroad and business center that she should be," individual businesses were delivered written solicitations by one hundred representatives of the chamber of commerce. Thirty of those monetary requests were given to Chinese grocers, and twenty-nine of them immediately contributed, with the one holdout saying that he'd pay within a few days. "The charge cannot be brought that the Chinese grocers in this city are not loyal to Tucson," stated the once Chinese-despising *Star*.

The EP&SW was welcomed to Tucson in late 1912, and a depot off south Main Street opened the following year. But the Phelps Dodge Corporation stopped its extension track-laying at Tucson and then sold the line to Southern Pacific in 1924. Its depot was closed, and all EP&SW trains began using the Southern Pacific station on Toole Avenue instead.

The line from Fairbank to Tucson, at least, actually got built. Meanwhile, the list of fictional railroad routes out of Tucson added another in 1907, when a proposal to lay tracks from town to the Santa Catalina Mountains to open "up one of the greatest gold mining districts in the world" was made. That pipe dream was joined the next year by a suggestion to run fourteen miles of track from Tucson to Sabino Canyon and then up the mountain to serve "the proposed scheme of building a summer resort at Mt. Lemmon." Neither of those projects, of course, ever got off the ground.

The railroad wasn't the only new transportation mode introduced during territorial times. A Herdic coach, a horse-drawn conveyance for twelve passengers, was operating by late 1881. This form of public transportation was followed in 1897 by a horse-drawn streetcar line that went from Main Street to the train station. A second line to the relatively new campus of the University of Arizona was added the following year. Around that time, the university had an enrollment of a few hundred, most of whom were high school students. The campus consisted primarily of one building finished in 1891, and in the years ahead, it would become known as "Old Main." In 1902, a streetcar line on south Fourth Avenue was also opened; in 1906, the routes were electrified. To improve the community even further, in 1907 the Southern Pacific Company replaced its original train station with a newer, larger, more architecturally pleasing structure.

Long before then, the dusty streets of Tucson had seen another newfangled contraption: a bicycle. A few velocipedes, or big front wheel bikes, were ordered by Tucson residents as early as 1869. The first regular bicycle was in town by 1880 and labeled an "inexpensive horse" by the *Citizen*. The newspaper added cautiously of these conveyances, "There seems to be but

The 1890s boom in bicycle riding brought several improvements, including in fashion, for women in Tucson and elsewhere. *Library of Congress, photo no. 29031.*

one objection to the bicycle—that it is unfitted for ladies use." The following years would prove the paper very wrong in that conclusion.

Despite wearing long dresses that must have made riding a severe challenge, a few women were on bicycles in Tucson, and in 1882, a bicycle club was established. The two-wheeled vehicle, however, remained a novelty for the next decade, with only sixteen of them being seen on city streets in 1892. The following year, however, saw an explosion of interest in bicycling both locally and nationally. "Before many days," the *Star* announced in September 1893, "everybody in town will be traveling on wheels. Tucson leads all cities in the country, of the same population, in number of bicycle riders." But the increase in cyclists quickly led to governmental regulations, with a speed limit set at six miles per hour and violators having to pay a seven-dollar fine. A requirement was also imposed that all bikes be equipped with a bell to be rung at every street corner. In response, one jokester "put a huge gong on his wheel [that was] eight inches in diameter."

Tucson's bicycling highlight of 1893 was undoubtedly the February visit of William L. Sachtleben and Thomas G. Allen Jr., two men from St. Louis who were close to completing a 'round-the-world excursion by bicycle. They had sailed to England in June 1890 and, after biking on the island, decided to keep going eastward. As winter set in, the two men reached Athens, and in the spring of 1891, they set off across Turkey and reached Mashad in Persia. From there they took a train to Tashkent, Russian Turkestan, where they spent the winter.

The following spring, the two men began to pedal across China, and by the end of 1892, they had sailed back to North America. Heading south and then east, the two were in Yuma, Arizona, by February 1, 1893, and told people that they were averaging fifty-five miles each day. After reaching the town of Maricopa south of Phoenix, the two were taken to the capital city by members of its bicycling club who "feted them, interviewed them, and otherwise made lions of them."

Upon reaching Tucson, Sachtleben and Allen were again wined and dined by local cycling enthusiasts as they recalled stories of their travel adventures. They departed town on February 8 and by June had reached New York City, completing their bicycling trek around the globe in thirty-six months.

The next two years would see women become the center of Tucson's, and the nation's, bicycling focus. Instead of wearing a long dress when riding, a local woman in May 1894 had on a "divided skirt," or bloomers, when she went pedaling one evening. Donning this pants-like dress was considered revolutionary in a time when the typical fashion for Anglo women in Tucson was "a chemise, a corset, a camisole and two petticoats under a long-sleeved serge [woolen cloth] dress." Mexican American women, on the other hand, usually wore comfortable clothing more suitable to the climate, including long cotton skirts.

It wasn't until November 1894 that a bloomers-wearing woman was seen riding in Tucson during daylight hours. Those at the *Star* indicated that this caused "a tremendous sensation" but calmly added, "All that is necessary is to wear off the novelty of the thing, and then a young lady attired in the much-discussed bloomers will attract no attention at all."

During the summer of 1895, Tucson was visited by another 'round-the-world cyclist, Annie Cohen Kopchovsky. She had taken up an 1894 wager that a woman couldn't bike around the world in fifteen months and raise $5,000 in the process. Leaving her husband and three children behind, she rode out of Boston on her way to Chicago in June 1894. In exchange for $100, she promoted the Londonderry Lithia Spring Water Company while calling herself "Annie Londonderry."

After reaching Chicago, Annie returned to the East Coast and in November sailed for France. Instead of bicycling, she took ships much of the way on her journey and by March 1895 was in San Francisco. From there she did pedal south and by June 20 had arrived in Tucson, where she told a *Star* reporter a very hard-to-believe hot weather story. Annie said that her bike had broken down in the California desert, "necessitating a walk and carrying of the broken wheel sixty-one miles to Yuma, taking her five days to make the trip." After giving a talk on her journey, she left Tucson and by September was in Chicago. She had completed the journey in less than the allotted time and had raised the mandated $5,000 through promotions and selling photos of herself—she reportedly then collected a $10,000 prize.

Even as Kopchovsky was crossing the country, *Harper's Bazaar* magazine, according to the *Citizen*, was advising women to take it easy on a bike:

> [I]*t ought to be a law for every woman that she should never ride a bicycle after a distinct feeling of weariness comes over her.*...*No ordinary woman who rides for pleasure once or twice a week should do over about ten miles at a time. This is perhaps an hour's ride.*...[N]*o woman can keep up a high rate of speed for even a generous portion of a mile and not create the beginnings of injury.*

Besides Kopchovsky's visit, more mundane Tucson bicycling activities during this period included a planned forty-mile trip in June 1894 that proved too much for six riders. The route chosen was over a sandy road, where "[t]ires sank out of sight, dust flew, and the heat of the sun was almost unbearable."

By the early '90s, in addition to frequent long-distance bicycle racing, short-course bicycle events were being held at the new Union Park, located at Twenty-Second Street and Park Avenue. In 1894, there was even a 4-mile race between a horse and bicyclist, with the bike rider having a 0.75-mile head start. Despite that, the horse won.

To accommodate even more short-course races, in 1895 the Tucson Cycle Club had a quarter-mile track built at Carrillo's Gardens south of downtown and near the Santa Cruz River. Other local riders, it was stated, "take an outing every morning between five and six o'clock on their wheels. They think nothing of a run of fifteen miles before breakfast." Among those regular riders was probably local physician Dr. Hiram Fenner. By 1894, it was said that he had purchased "one of the finest bicycles in Tucson" and was "becoming quite a bicyclist."

But just as the 1890s bicycling craze in the United States and Tucson had appeared unexpectedly, it faded quickly. In southern Arizona, that change was signaled at the end of 1899 when Dr. Fenner purchased the first locally owned auto, a "Locomobile," for $800. It was a "two-person, steam-powered

Dr. Hiram Fenner imported the first locally owned automobile, a Locomobile like this one, to Tucson in December 1899. *Library of Congress, photo no. 118656.*

vehicle, which had one tank for five gallons of gasoline and another for 16 gallons of water."

In 1902, Locomobiles were replaced by Oldsmobiles. Four of the new vehicles were sold in one week alone. By 1910, a "Hupmobile" was being offered for sale at $850, and that same year, Fred Ronstadt, who had emigrated from Mexico to Tucson years before to learn the wagon making business, was selling both the "Flanders 20" and the "E-M-F 30" models of automobiles from his shop.

The growing number of cars on local streets, with 196 being licensed by 1910, led the *Star* to proclaim in a headline, "Old Pueblo Is a City of Automobiles." The speeding of up to twenty miles an hour by cars, it was pointed out, would invariably lead to accidents. One of the earliest was in 1906 at the intersection of Stone Avenue and Broadway between an automobile and a streetcar. "The chauffeur, George A. Wells," the *Citizen* stated of the automobile driver, "was hurled from his car and severely injured about the head. The automobile was almost a complete wreck." To reduce the risk, a city ordinance was adopted that the speed limit for automobiles would be seven miles per hour.

For sale in 1910 for $850, this Hupmobile shows the numerous design changes made to autos in a decade. *Photo by F.D. Richards, 2013, Wikimedia Commons.*

It wasn't only potential accidents that Tucson's small number of automobile drivers had to contend with early in the twentieth century. Even though by 1911 long-distance travel by car was beginning to replace railroad trips for some businessmen, they had few roads to drive over that were not just dirt trails; also, the machines they rode in were anything but reliable. Illustrating those problems, in 1908 four men set out in a Pope-Hartford car intent on making the round trip from town to the San Xavier Mission in one hour. They were on schedule and headed back to Tucson when the car gave out, the driver lost control and they "started to climb through a cactus thicket up the side of the hill." The four then dejectedly walked back to town.

Around that time, both short- and long-distance automobile races were being held. In 1907, a four-mile race was driven on "The Speedway," and by 1911, that dirt street had become part of a fourteen-mile course that saw more races.

Local auto enthusiasts J. Knox Corbett, a businessman, and his son, Hiram ("Hi"), won a six-car Tucson-to-Phoenix race in 1908. On New Year's Day 1911, the winner of a Phoenix-to-Tucson race covered the 138-mile distance in about four hours and forty minutes, an average of almost 30 miles per hour. Three years earlier, H.D. Hayes decided to take a more leisurely drive to Phoenix from Tucson. He made the 1908 trip in twelve hours and twenty minutes. It was a very slow start to the radical change that was taking place in personal transportation.

Chapter 4

PRESIDENTIAL VISITS

Before dawn on October 24, 1880, a special train departed from Tucson's recently completed depot. Heading north, the train was ferrying a few dozen of the community's most important men to meet a very special guest to Arizona: the nineteenth president of the United States, Rutherford B. Hayes.

While almost 65 percent of Tucson's population of 7,007 were Mexican Americans, only a handful of those on the train were of Mexican descent. They included Leopoldo Carrillo, Mariano Samaniego and Carlos Velasco.

Originally from Sonora, Mexico, Leopoldo Carrillo had come to Tucson at age twenty-three in 1859. He was involved with freighting, ranching, rental property and numerous other small businesses. But it was his recreational development near the Santa Cruz River, begun a few years after Hayes's visit, which was his lasting legacy. "Carrillo's Gardens," Thomas Sheridan noted in *Los Tucsoneses*, "eight acres of rose gardens, fruit trees, and man-made lakes, [was] Tucson's crowning glory in the late nineteenth century."

The thirty-six-year-old Mariano Samaniego had also been born in Sonora, but at an early age he immigrated to the United States. Over time, his business interests would include freighting, ranching, stage lines and water supply. Additionally, he was a frequent member of elected governmental bodies.

When he met Hayes, Carlos Velasco was the forty-three-year-old publisher of Tucson's *El Fronterizo* newspaper. Also from Sonora, he settled in Tucson in 1877 and established the paper the following year. His intention for the Spanish-language publication was to have it be "the jealous defender of the

President Rutherford B. Hayes and Lucy Webb Hayes visited Tucson in October 1880. *Library of Congress, photo no. 126421.*

interests of Mexicans in both countries, expressing their opinions and directing their initiative along the path of moral improvement and material progress."

At 9:30 a.m. in Casa Grande on the twenty-fourth, the Tucson gentlemen greeted Hayes and his small party, which included his wife, Lucy Webb Hayes; their son, Rutherford Platt Hayes; Secretary of War Alexander Ramsey; and Commander of the Army William T. Sherman. When elected president in 1876, Hayes committed to serving only one term. Thus, in late August 1880, with Congress not in session, he departed Washington, D.C., intent on seeing the Pacific coastline, as well as other western parts of the country. Having traveled mostly by train but also using numerous other types of conveyance, by the time the Hayes party left Los Angeles and reached Arizona on their way home, the presidential group had been on the road for two months.

As the president's train moved south from Casa Grande, Hayes conversed with some of the Tucson men, including Velasco, who gave him a recent copy of his newspaper. In his report on the conversation, Velasco stated:

> *The President speaks some Spanish and he reads it with ease....He read a few paragraphs of* [Mexican dictator Porfirio] *Diaz's speech at the inauguration of the 10th National Congress and was pleased with the peace and progress of Mexico. He also read part of the article "New Americans" and some other paragraphs, and of all of them spoke to us as one who understands what he reads well.*

Meanwhile, Sherman was holding forth on various topics, including the American Indian Wars. He stated that when the nation's second transcontinental rail line was finished in a few months, "the Indian problem will have been solved as far as you in Arizona are concerned." To that incorrect prognostication, a Globe, Arizona newspaper replied, "Gen. Sherman thinks the railway settles the Indian question. We think it would, if a fence were built each side of the track, and the Indians kept between them."

The presidential party and welcoming committee arrived in Tucson at 12:30 p.m. and were greeted by thousands of cheering people. One man in the crowd, however, yelled out a derogatory comment about Hayes's controversial 1876 election.

Horse-drawn carriages took the national and local dignitaries on a brief community tour and then stopped for a reception, lunch and general conversation at the imposing Victorian-style home of local merchant William W. Williams. Following another short excursion on the town's dirt streets, the group returned to the depot, where Hayes, Ramsey and Sherman offered brief remarks. "Endeavor to have such good schools," the public education–supporting president told the assembled crowd, "that the rich cannot do better than to send their children to them and the poor will have as good educational advantages as any."

After a visit of four hours, Hayes's train steamed out of town eastward. Among the many people involved with the gala gathering had been about one hundred Papago Indians, who shook the president's hand while he was at the Williams home.

Having long lived in the region, a 1985 tribal history prepared by the Tohono O'odham Nation stated of their ancestors, "They had their own economy based on the resources of the land. They were able gatherers, hunters, farmers,

President Hayes might have seen south Meyer Street, shown here, on his brief Tucson tour. *Library of Congress, HABS ARIZ, 10-TUCSO, 30–7.*

Along with farming and ranching, Papago (Tohono O'odham) tribal members made pots and baskets while also harvesting desert plants. *National Archives, photo no. 532042.*

and traders. The O'odham relied on themselves. The people made what they needed: houses, baskets, clothing, tools, and sacred objects."

For twenty years following the Gadsden Purchase, the relationship between the Papagos and arriving European American settlers was often cordial, even though the native people were sometimes belittled by the newcomers. In 1859, the *Weekly Arizonian* newspaper stated, "As we write these lines, half-a-dozen Papagos are clustered around our door, muttering their disagreeable guttural language, their stupid countenances, exhibiting no sign nor symptom of thought or emotion." In the same article, the newspaper wrote of all Native Americans, "[B]y experience [we] have learned to regard the Indian in his true character, a worthless, impracticable, relentless barbarian, who is absolutely incapable of civilization…disappearing before the steady domination of the Saxon race, as it is right and proper he should do."

Despite that racist sentiment, Papagos were usually perceived as friendly toward European Americans, in part because of their common dislike for the Apaches. The depredations by all sides would reach a low point on April 30, 1871. Organized by William S. Oury, Granville's brother, and led by rancher Jesús Maria Elias, ninety-four Papagos, forty-eight Mexican Americans and six European Americans set out from Tucson, seeking bloody revenge for Apache atrocities. Armed with rifles and ammunition supplied by local businessman Sam Hughes, the group attacked a camp supposedly under U.S. Army protection near Camp Grant along Aravaipa Creek about fifty miles north of town. But instead of killing Apache warriors, they massacred more than one hundred people, nearly all of whom were women and children. They also took almost thirty children away, many to be sold into slavery in Mexico, although some were kept by families in Tucson. When the perpetrators went on trial, it took the jury just nineteen minutes to find them not guilty. Despite the massacre, the killings and stealing by both sides didn't stop.

In 1874, the Papagos living near the San Xavier Mission were allocated a 111-square-mile reservation by the U.S. government, but the vast majority of tribal members resided on traditional but unsecured land north or west of Tucson, as well as in Mexico. At San Xavier, stock raising was the primary occupation, while women created *ollas* (water carrying clay jugs) of different sizes as well as baskets and tableware to sell in Tucson. Barley, wheat and corn were raised for both their own consumption as well as to sell. Vegetables, such as beans and squash, were grown, and the fruit of desert plants was harvested. Venison, chickens from thirty to fifty cents each and wood were sold by the Papagos; occasionally, they also had both salt and gold mined in Mexico.

For decades, Apache warriors battled European Americans, Mexican Americans and Papagos. *National Archives, photo no. 530902.*

Plus, members of the tribe sometimes provided entertainment in town, with the San Xavier Raw Hide Band appearing annually at a celebration held at Levin's Park. This was a three-acre entertainment area west of downtown established by German Jewish émigré Alex Levin in the 1870s. It preceded Carrillo's Gardens and was also located near the Santa Cruz River.

Life on their reservation was obviously hard, and many Papagos were extremely poor. Occasionally, some of them got drunk in Tucson. In addition, sometimes they didn't have access to medical treatment on the reservation because a government-provided physician wasn't always available. But about forty Papago children attended a mission school established in 1864 at San Xavier, and twenty years later it was written of the students, "Their disposition to learn is remarkable, and a pupil is never absent unless prevented from attending by cause of sickness." The following year, the *Citizen* in 1885 stated of the Papagos, "They fully realize that the influx of white people has brought them more money and comforts than they ever had before in all their lives: by furnishing a market for all they have to dispose of, by giving them employment."

But in the 1880s, conflicts began happening between Papagos and European American ranchers. The latter started trespassing onto land traditionally used by the Indians and then claiming that the Papagos were stealing their cattle.

Numerous Papagos also shook hands with the next president to visit Tucson, Benjamin Harrison, during his brief visit in April 1891. But they

President Benjamin Harrison, shown with Caroline Scott Harrison, commented on statehood for Arizona during his brief 1891 Tucson visit. *Library of Congress, photo no. 32402.*

were children enrolled in the three-year-old Indian School, operated by the Presbyterian Church. The school, out by the university campus, was trying to teach the pupils "useful" skills such as religion, farming techniques and English. "The children know nothing at all in the line of self-support. Nor do their parents for that matter," the school's superintendent, Howard Billman, wrote of the native people who had lived in the area for centuries.

A few years after that, about five hundred people resided on the San Xavier reservation. To provide more land for the tribe, proposals were made in the early 1890s to create another reservation west of Tucson, but these ideas were opposed by local politicians and ranchers. The *Star* labeled the land suggested to be allocated for a reservation "one of the most valuable grazing sections of southern Pima [County]." The newspaper also called for simply moving all of the hundreds of Papagos living in the county to San Xavier and forcing them to become farmers. With opposition like that, it wasn't surprising that the idea of creating another, larger reservation for the tribe went nowhere for several decades.

President Harrison's westbound train stopped for only thirty-five minutes at the Tucson station, where he was greeted by thousands of people and the loud ringing of church bells. He heard a welcoming address from U.S. Attorney for Arizona Thomas F. Wilson. With the American Indian Wars having ended in 1886 after Geronimo's surrender, and Tucson's military post, Fort Lowell, closing around the time of Harrison's visit, Wilson talked of the new top priority for many territorial residents: statehood. Harrison in reply said to great applause, "If Arizona has the qualifications [for statehood] and I am then president, I shall take pleasure in signing a bill admitting it as a state."

Trying to force the statehood issue, a few months later, Arizona politicians in September 1891 convened a constitutional convention. They prepared a conservative, business-oriented document but rejected women's suffrage by a vote of sixteen to five. When placed before the territory's voters, the draft state constitution was adopted with the supportive vote in Tucson being by an overwhelming seven-to-one margin. But this early effort to pressure Congress into granting statehood to Arizona found little backing from national leaders, and the measure went nowhere.

Ignoring the Arizona statehood issue continued to be the situation when President William McKinley's train rolled into Tucson in May 1901. It was an eight-car special that included a barbershop, a smoking room and the president's car, "The Olympia," which had an enormous brass bed. Accompanied by his wife, Ida Saxton McKinley, as well as Secretary of the Interior Ethan A. Hitchcock and Secretary of Agriculture James Wilson, McKinley would also spend only thirty-five minutes in town.

Several prominent local men met with Secretary Wilson for part of that time. Informed that leading citizens of Phoenix wanted to take federal agricultural funding away from the University of Arizona in order to develop an agricultural school in the capital city, they sought to put the kibosh on that idea and succeeded.

Before the presidential visit, the Republican-loyal *Arizona Daily Citizen* had editorialized, "William McKinley is by no means one of the greatest of the Presidents." Despite that blunt observation, at least three thousand people gathered at the depot to see him, and he spoke for a few minutes, focusing on the nation's military accomplishments as well as its economic prosperity. "The President touched upon the country he had seen [on his trip] and how favorably it impressed him," reported the *Citizen*, "but he got no further toward the great question which is the foundation of Arizona's ambition.… [T]he word Statehood never came from his lips."

McKinley was assassinated a few months later, and his successor, Theodore Roosevelt, had an unusual idea for addressing the Arizona statehood issue. Seeking to limit the number of Democrats in the U.S. Senate, since Arizona

President William McKinley didn't mention statehood during his 1901 stop in Tucson; Theodore Roosevelt as president proposed joint statehood. *Library of Congress, photo no. 3986.*

was definitely a Democratic-leaning territory, Roosevelt proposed early in his presidency that Arizona and New Mexico be combined into one state. Since the capital would be in Santa Fe and the majority of people resided in New Mexico, many people there supported the idea. But the sentiment in Arizona was extremely antagonistic. The concept, however, was placed on the ballot in both territories during 1906. It passed in New Mexico with 64 percent favoring joint statehood, but the measure failed by more than a five-to-one margin in Arizona.

That outcome, of course, came from mostly white male voters. Women couldn't vote. Neither could Native Americans, who wouldn't even be considered citizens until 1924. Almost none of Tucson's Chinese residents could vote either. If they were immigrants, they couldn't even become citizens since the Chinese Exclusion Act of May 1882 specifically forbade it. While both African American and Mexican American males could theoretically cast ballots, steps such as requiring payment of a poll tax in order to vote had been put in place to discourage their participation. These voting suppression techniques would be further strengthened in 1909, when a voter literacy requirement was adopted.

With rejection of joint statehood, Arizona remained a territory. There was an outlandish idea put forth in 1907 to combine Arizona with the existing state of Nevada; two years later, some people in California, with a straight face, talked about linking Arizona with Imperial County to form the new state of Imperial. That far-fetched scheme was soon followed by the absurd idea to join Arizona with the counties of Southern California to create a new state whose capital would be Los Angeles.

The people of Tucson and Arizona were having nothing to do with those harebrained schemes. They wanted statehood for themselves, and in June 1910, Congress finally offered them the opportunity to get it as a stand-alone state. Another Arizona constitutional convention was called, but this one was dominated by mostly Democratic, liberal-leaning, labor-supporting delegates. They prepared a document that was in several respects extremely progressive for its time yet still rejected women's suffrage. The draft constitution did provide voters the power to recall all elected officials, to refer adopted laws to the electorate and to place items directly on the ballot through an initiative process.

President William H. Taft indicated that he wasn't happy with the recall provision since it would impact elected judges, and he felt strongly that they should be immune from political pressure. Ignoring those signals, Arizona voters overwhelmingly approved the constitution in February 1911, with Tucson voters supporting it by 867 to 350. The measure then went to Congress for approval. It passed there, but Taft vetoed the statehood bill, stating that the recall of judges had to be removed from the constitution. That was done in a December 1911 special election by a 7-to-1 margin, and Arizona finally became a state on February 14, 1912. Snubbing Taft, nine months later the voters of the forty-eighth state placed the recall of judges back into Arizona's constitution. At the same time, they granted women the right to vote, eight years before that was done nationally.

Long before then, the *Tucson Citizen* had outlined what it thought statehood would mean for Arizona. The grass wouldn't be greener or the rainfall greater, the newspaper predicted of the impact, "but more people and more money to make the best use of the present resources which nature has given Arizona" would certainly result.

Chapter 5

CELEBRATIONS GALORE

Statehood day in Tucson was actually somewhat restrained. Church bells did ring and whistles did blow when President Taft signed the proclamation on February 14, 1912. At the University of Arizona, military cadets paraded, and some speeches were made, with one orator optimistically predicting of the forty-eighth state, "It will be inhabited by the happiest, prosperous and most contented citizenship of any commonwealth in the union."

The earlier celebration to mark the start of the twentieth century on January 1, 1900, had also been fairly subdued. The privately owned local water company illuminated its eight-story, downtown reservoir, a dinner and dance were put on by the Order of Railway Conductors and a midnight mass was held at the relatively new Catholic cathedral on Stone Avenue.

A low-key celebration had certainly not been the case when the United States commemorated its 100th anniversary of declaring independence. The Fourth of July 1876 was grandly celebrated across the country, including in the remote community of Tucson. Flags hung everywhere, and the *Citizen* proudly crowed, "It is safe to say that no town in the United States—size considered, made a more liberal display of bunting." The festivities, under the leadership of past and future mayor James H. Toole, began with a parade that wound throughout the center of town. Stretching for at least half a mile in length, the marchers were led by the Sixth Cavalry band from Camp Lowell. They were followed by six horses pulling a wagon carrying one hundred young women representing the centennial. Also included in

The centennial celebration was a major event across the nation, including in remote Tucson. *Library of Congress, photo no. 05034.*

the parade were a group of Mexican American citizens in uniforms, another wagon hauled by horses with representatives of the four human races ("Caucasian, Ethiopian, Mongolian, and Indian") aboard and at the rear came citizens in carriages, on horseback or walking.

The parade disbanded at Levin's Park near the Santa Cruz River, and the Declaration of Independence was read in both English and Spanish. Speeches in the two languages were also delivered. Complying with a Congressional resolution that every town in the nation should hear a history of that community on this special Fourth, early educator John Spring gave the keynote address. Focusing on Tucson's twenty-two-year-old American history, in his lengthy speech Spring said of the post–Civil War period, "With the year 1866, it may be said the golden era of prosperity commenced for Arizona and especially for Tucson." After dark, people returned to the park for a dance, while a few blocks away a huge bonfire burned, accompanied by fireworks; many homes throughout town used candles or Chinese lanterns for illumination. "It was the finest celebration I ever saw in this town," concluded saloonkeeper George Hand in his diary.

Celebrating America's birthday would naturally be marked every year. But Tucson's population was a diverse blend of peoples, all of whom had their own ceremonies and festivals. Despite that, Pittsburgh's *Chronicle Telegraph* newspaper predicted in 1890 of the community: "[W]hat will be the future of this odd mixture of Chinese, Mexican, Indian, and American people? Of course it will only have one answer—it will become all American."

That forecast certainly proved incorrect for festivities, with every ethnic group of any size either continuing preexisting ceremonies or initiating new ones. As an example, the first cathedral constructed outside the presidio walls was completed south of Congress Street around 1860. The church was fronted by a large plaza where "The Feast," an annual weeklong celebration attended mostly by Mexican American Catholics, was held. The celebration honored St. Augustine, namesake of the church, and incorporated both religious and secular events. An 1869 description said that following a church service, lovely *señoritas* and *caballeros* would gather to dance the night away.

To remember Mexico's 1810 declaration of independence from Spain, Tucson's Mexican American community celebrated annually, and in 1876, it held a two-day festival. Put on at Levin's Park, the first day's activities included an oration, performances by two bands and fireworks. The next day had a parade that included a wagon carrying twenty-seven young women representing each state of Mexico, more speeches and a second night of fireworks.

The centennial of this important date in Mexican history was celebrated in even grander style on September 16, 1910. The day began with short speeches in front of the Mexican consulate on Pennington Street, followed by tunes from the brass and drum Old Pueblo Band. Sporting events, including a sack race and attempts to climb a greased pole, preceded a parade, band concert, more speeches in English and Spanish and a dance attended by at least one hundred couples.

This annual celebration had been joined in the 1870s by a Cinco de Mayo (May 5) commemoration marking the Mexican victory against French troops at the 1862 Battle of Puebla. Carlos Velasco, in an 1879 issue of *El Fronterizo* newspaper, observed that the day was held "with all the splendor possible." He spoke at the event and music was played, followed by a lunch at Levin's Park attended by more than one hundred people. A dance concluded the day's activities.

Celebrating Mexican Independence Day on September 16, 1905. *Arizona Historical Society, #44623.*

Cinco de Mayo continued to be celebrated annually by Tucson's Mexican Americans, but in 1910, the event was transformed into a gigantic, promotional, two-day extravaganza marking the completion of the Tucson & West Coast of Mexico Railroad. The city's population, nearly 13,000 primarily European Americans by then, was reportedly doubled by visitors who came to see the spectacle. The first day's activities began with a parade with 3,500 marchers, with the *Star* exclaiming, "Two hours before the parade yesterday morning, the streets of Tucson were lined with the greatest throng of humanity ever known here." While many of the parade participants had no connection to Mexico, there was a thirty-five-piece band from Hermosillo, Sonora, along with a Porfirio Díaz Society float honoring the long-serving Mexican dictator. Also involved were marchers from the Americano-Mexicano Society and the Spanish-American Society.

The parade highlight for many people, however, was participation for the first time by Tucson's small Chinese community, which had raised $1,500 to bring a giant gold and silver silk dragon from San Francisco. The Chinese contingent was led by gong beaters, men waving banners and chariots "bearing small Chinese boys and girls gaudily dressed and painted to represent Chinese rulers and deities." Following them came twenty men carrying the dragon, described as a "huge, glaring, writhing object, glistening and fanged with red tongues lashing about the famous image." The *Citizen* proclaimed the Chinese display "almost indescribable." After the parade, a free barbecue lunch for five thousand people was put on at Elysian Grove, the renamed successor facility of Carrillo's Gardens, and in the evening a formal banquet for two hundred was held. The next day, to no one's surprise, the Chinese were awarded $100 "for making the best showing in the parade."

The celebration of the Chinese in 1910 certainly wasn't their first in Tucson. By the early 1880s, they annually observed Chinese New Year in January or February with loud firecrackers and jubilant rejoicing. In 1896, Chinese New Year attracted a large, diverse audience to Tucson's Chinatown near Main Street and was described as "religious fires burned in every [Chinese] store and laundry. A kind of Chinese whiskey seductive in taste and powerful in its influence was as free as water. Many Americans [*sic*] drank copiously of it and then became a part of the celebration."

There were lots of other Chinese celebrations throughout the territorial period, some serious and others happenstance. Celebrating an 1885 Chinese battlefield victory in the Franco-Chinese War, an April event involved "[s]lips of papers on which were inscribed thanks offerings to their gods [being] strewn to the winds while numerous candles were lighted." In 1887, sarcastically boasting that they were holding a celebration in March "because the Arizona legislature had adjourned without abolishing the Chinese empire," Tucson's Chinese set off a loud display of firecrackers. Then, in 1893, an October event was attended by almost all of the approximately three hundred Chinese residents of town. Taking up an entire city block, it included a pig and chicken roast at one end and a bonfire at the other. Between them were two rows of dirt piles, each holding lit torches. A "priest" overseeing the festivities was dressed in elaborate garb, including a pink gown, a white sash and a flaming red headdress. When asked what the occasion was, an attendee told a *Citizen* reporter, "None of your business."

The year 1893 was also when Louis C. Hughes, the Chinese-hating publisher of the *Arizona Daily Star*, was appointed territorial governor. He served for three years, and when he was replaced in 1896, Tucson's Chinese constructed a high scaffolding and "three strings of crackers and bombs [were] suspended therefrom." The resultant loud display gleefully celebrated Hughes's departure from office.

Texas slaves were finally freed on June 19, 1865. That date was later celebrated annually by African Americans nationwide. *Library of Congress, photo no. 03898.*

Not celebrating in 1903 was a Chinese man wishing to wed a Mexican American woman. They were informed by a judge that "the [1865 territorial] laws on miscegenation forbid the union of the Mongol and the Caucasian." Instead, the judge urged the couple to go to Mexico to complete their union.

For their part, Tucson's small population of African Americans also celebrated. By the end of the nineteenth century, they were marking the day on June 19 in 1865 when news of the end of slavery finally reached the former Confederate state of Texas. An annual event commemorating "Juneteenth" began, and in 1908, a well-attended gathering was held along the Rillito Creek north of the city that included "speaking, shooting matches and baseball, foot races and dancing." Two years later, the celebration was at the Elysian Grove recreation area, but the day began with an automobile float "loaded with children…[and] decorated in the national colors and flags" parading through the city. The evening's program included songs such as "America" and "Steal Away to Jesus," performed by the Old Pueblo Band, along with a speech entitled "Conditions Since Emancipation." Among those attending to give a goodwill greeting was Louis C. Hughes, whose *Star* newspaper years earlier had endorsed not having Black soldiers serve in Arizona.

Tucson's African American residents also participated in the solemn August 8, 1885 observance of the burial of former president and U.S. army general Ulysses S. Grant. A legal holiday was declared, so banks, the post office and stores were closed, while a bell tolled throughout the day. For their part, Tucson's African Americans were honoring the man they acknowledged was, in large part, responsible for bringing them "the blessings of liberty."

It was a lack of liberty that in the late nineteenth century drove Yaqui Indians north across the American border from their traditional Mexican homelands. That region, surrounding the Yaqui River in central and southern Sonora, Mexico, was described as an "idyllic country…in which children played alongside the river, of fields where watermelons, beans, sweet potatoes, bananas, and sugarcane grew in abundance." But Yaqui desire to preserve the autonomy they had enjoyed for almost 150 years was forcefully opposed by Mexican officials beginning in 1885. That is when Mexican president Porfirio Díaz was informed that his military should "definitely subjugate and pacify these Indians to the obedience of the government."

The subsequent violence forced some Yaquis to flee on foot hundreds of miles north to cross the border and establish small communities in Arizona. By 1906, the Mexicans had declared "a war of extermination" against any Yaqui who didn't surrender to face relocation to the distant Yucatan peninsula. As a result, the estimated Yaqui population in Sonora dropped from twenty thousand in 1885 to fewer than three thousand by 1907. That was the year the U.S. government finally granted Yaquis political asylum.

There was a Yaqui "colony" in Tucson by 1908, and soon tribal members would be living together in small settlements both north and south of downtown. The next few years saw some semblance of peace restored to Sonora, even as the Mexican Revolution eventually broke out. Yaquis continued to cross the border, and an armed group of them was stopped south of Tucson in 1910 by law enforcement. After a conference involving U.S. immigration officials, it was decided that no action would be taken and "[t]he Indians will be let alone unless they commit some act which will render them liable to prosecution, which they have not done thus far."

Despite lingering animosity between the Yaquis and the Mexican government, to mark the centennial of Mexico's declaration of independence from Spain, it was surprisingly decided in 1910 to invite a Yaqui group to put on a "war dance" at Tucson's Mexican Independence Day celebration. One man did perform, accompanied by a violin and harp, and the next year in Tucson, Yaquis in larger numbers celebrated San Juan Day, the traditional late June arrival of life-giving desert summer rains.

With the Mexican government trying to subjugate them, Yaquis, perhaps including this woman, fled north across the U.S. border. *Library of Congress, photo no. 104492.*

Several miles to the south of town, San Xavier Mission was the site of many Papago celebrations. One of the earliest reported on was in 1876, marking the feast day of San Francis Xavier, patron saint of the church. It was a two-day event that involved "bull-fights, horse and foot racing, dancing, etc."

Another type of festival was held at the mission on Palm Sunday in April 1884. "Many Papagos and Mexicans were present," the *Star* stated, and "each held in their hand a young stalk of green corn, which, as one of them afterwards explained, was made to possess wonderful curative powers….It was likewise to be used as an invoker of rain when such was desired."

West of town that same year, at the mining camp of Quijotoa, an Easter ceremony was held one week later. Up to two hundred Papago men sat around a campfire, surrounded by women holding children. In the center of this crowd were masked dancers, "their waists encircled with empty, jingling cartridge shells, their ankles bound with rattlesnake bangles," moving to the sounds of musicians playing flutes, drums and violins.

While many of Tucson's territorial celebrations were held by one individual ethnic group or another, the May 15 feast day of San Ysidro, the

Mission San Xavier del Bac, circa 1870, has graced southern Arizona for more than two centuries. *Library of Congress, photo no. 3g05666.*

patron saint of fields and crops, traditionally brought together all farmers and ranchers. In 1894, with financial assistance from the Chinese, an image of the saint was carried by Mexican Americans in a procession around each of the agricultural fields along the Santa Cruz River. "At every house [along the way], refreshments are on hand and are served," wrote the *Citizen*.

This event, like most of Tucson's celebrations, was peaceful and without incident. But occasionally, the exuberance of a holiday led to injuries. Such was the case in 1911 at the community's Fourth of July fireworks display. A man was hit on the head by a piece of ordnance; also, according to the *Star*, a boy "picked up a rocket which had not exploded, and the missile went off in his hand. The hand was badly shattered and will probably be lost." Fortunately, by then, those injuries could be treated at Tucson's growing number of healthcare facilities.

Chapter 6

A HEALTH RESORT

With the long elusive dream of statehood for Arizona about to be realized in early 1912, Tucson and its more than thirteen thousand residents could boast of two hospitals, a few sanitariums for tubercular patients and several other health-related facilities. It also had nineteen male physicians, a woman doctor and eight dentists.

The medical situation had been radically different fifty-two years earlier. With fewer than one thousand people, Tucson in 1860 had only two doctors; a decade later, it had three when the population exceeded three thousand. To treat the seven thousand people in town by 1880, the number of physicians was nine.

While small military hospitals had previously existed, Tucson in 1880 finally had its first full-service civilian hospital. Prior to that, "hospital" stays were in a boardinghouse-type arrangement. The location of this "County Hospital" moved frequently from place to place, while those with contagious diseases such as smallpox were sent to a "pest house."

Dramatically changing that less than desirable situation, on May 1, 1880, the twelve-bed St. Mary's Hospital on the west side of the Santa Cruz River admitted its first eleven patients. Founded by Bishop Jean-Baptiste Salpointe, the institution would be staffed by four nuns: sisters Basil Morris, St. Martin Dunn, Julia Ford and Mary John Noli. They belonged to the order of St. Joseph of Carondelet, which in 1870 had sent its first group of seven other nuns on a difficult thirty-six-day overland journey from Missouri to open an academy for girls in Tucson.

To pay for the much-needed hospital, Bishop Salpointe in April 1879 approached both the Tucson City Council and Pima County Board of Supervisors for financial assistance. The latter, however, rejected his request with regret because "under their legal authority they could not act in the premises." A group of prominent men—including Estevan Ochoa, William Oury, Mariano Samaniego and Ochoa's freight company business partner, Pinckney R. Tully—thus formed the Benevolent Society of St. Mary's. Their intention was to raise the capital needed to build and operate the hospital. The mission of the institution was that "[i]ts benefits will be conferred alike upon the sick and destitute of all creeds, colors, and conditions."

By the end of June 1879, Ochoa and Tully had each contributed $1,000, a substantial portion of the total amount needed, and a fundraising dance was also planned for August, with tickets costing $5. As the nearly six-thousand-square-foot building was being erected in September, Ochoa chauffeured a *Citizen* reporter to the distant site. The hospital was made of stone quarried from a nearby mountain and stood two stories high with an attic. "The entire structure is well arranged for ventilation, convenience and durability," concluded the newspaper's report.

Upon its 1880 opening, St. Mary's was almost immediately full of patients, but water had to be hand-carried from the nuns' convent quite a distance away. Responding to this shortcoming, the *Citizen* launched a drive to raise money to erect a windmill near the hospital to pump water for both humans and vegetation. As was customary, a benefit dance at Levin's Park was held, with Ochoa and Tully acting as treasurers. The money raised by the dance, $102, contributed to the $400 total required, and the windmill was later installed.

The patients at St. Mary's quickly fell into three categories. There were those who could pay their own way. The second group comprised injured railroad employees whom Southern Pacific covered. Indigent patients, whose bills the county government was responsible for paying, composed the third group. From its opening, words of praise were heaped on both the nuns and the hospital by former patients and governmental inspectors alike. Thomas Hughes, chair of the county's 1887 hospital committee, observed that "the Sisters are deserving of great credit for their untiring devotions to the sick of the county."

Despite the kind words, the hospital's rapid expansion—doubling in size in 1882, with another addition two years later increasing capacity to fifty patients—led to shaky finances. Since a high percentage of patients were poor and their daily expenses had to be paid by the county government,

St. Mary's hospital had both a windmill (*left*) and a tubercular facility (*right*) by 1900. *Arizona Historical Society, #24788.*

the three-member Pima County Board of Supervisors had decided by 1882 to require their approval for every indigent admission. This meant that many people might not be admitted simply because neither they nor the county could afford the typical hospital cost of a few dollars per day. With the county providing about $8,000 annually for indigent care in the early 1880s, the *Citizen* reported on a "wounded Indian woman" who sought admission to St. Mary's. Since she was poor and neither a U.S. citizen nor a taxpayer, she was refused entry by the board of supervisors, but two generous people fortunately pledged to pay her bill. In 1893, however, the board did allow the admittance of a penniless Mexican man who had accidentally shot himself in the leg.

Among the nuns serving at St. Mary's after it opened was Sister M. Immaculate. "She was a bright woman," the *Star* wrote at the time of her death in 1894, "loved by all with whom she came in contact." The cause of her death, like many others in Tucson, was tuberculosis. When contracted, this dreadful disease had symptoms of "fatigue, weight loss and night sweats, followed by pallor with flushed cheeks." Thus, it became known as consumption, or the white plague. Eventually, coughing up sputum and later hemorrhaging from the lungs could lead to the sufferer becoming painfully incapacitated and eventually dying.

To increase its population, Tucson promoted itself as a health resort for tuberculosis patients. *American National Red Cross, 1919, Library of Congress, photo no. 43100.*

As early as 1874, six years before the arrival of the railroad, Tucson's climate was being offered as possible relief from tuberculosis. In an article entitled "A Word to Consumptives," the *Citizen* declared, "Far be it from us to desire to entice any poor sufferer to come here for selfish purposes, but if the climate is such that nearly everyone gets relief, and those not too far gone are cured, then it is an act of humanity to let these facts be known."

While Tucson's climate was described as health restoring across several decades, death notices from tuberculosis occasionally did appear in local newspapers. Many of these people had migrated to Tucson, but others were longtime residents like Ygnacio Gonzales. He was the bookkeeper of a local business, a member of the Spanish-American Alliance and played with the Philharmonic band led by Fred Ronstadt. Upon Ygnacio's death from tuberculosis in 1895, he left behind a widow and one child.

Setbacks like those didn't prevent many physicians from suggesting southern Arizona as a destination for their tubercular patients. Dr. N.C. Glasgow of St. Louis was quoted in 1895 as saying, "I fully appreciate the Tucson climate and I have been sending patients there for ten years. Some have improved, many have died, but on the whole I consider it the best place for chronic phthisis [tuberculosis] in the country." A Tucson doctor, N.H. Matas, countered that opinion two years later. "It is our advice, therefore," he told the *Star*, "to those who are too far gone, to stay at home, rather than to die far away among strangers seeking vainly a change of climate."

By the end of the nineteenth century, about 20 percent of the 216 total annual deaths in Tucson had been caused by tuberculosis. Without other hope, people with the disease in all stages kept coming to town, yet many perished nonetheless. One of those was James W. Lytle, an aspiring lawyer from Ohio. He had been in Tucson for two years, but eventually his health declined in late 1898. On one of the last evenings of his life, he was taken outdoors and, looking up at the moon, exclaimed, "How beautiful is this night."

With numerous tuberculosis sufferers continuing to head to southern Arizona despite medical warnings that the climate wasn't a guaranteed cure, the *Star* in 1905 nonetheless returned to the theme of Tucson's weather being life-saving. "The climate is the most effective germicide [a germ destroying agent] anywhere to be found in the United States," the newspaper claimed. "Hundreds upon hundreds of those restored to health and spared from what seemed an early death attest the truth of the fact that the Tucson basin and its tributary points is without an equal as the region where the pulmonary disease cannot live or thrive."

Unsubstantiated promotional statements like that continued to be refuted by some in the medical profession. As local doctor, A. Morrison, straightforwardly wrote in 1908, "Climate alone cannot perform miracles.... It is criminal for physicians to send patients here or elsewhere with insufficient means for proper support."

But people with tuberculosis kept coming, even though adequate accommodations to house them were generally not available. The need for a sanitarium for health seekers had been pointed out by the *Star* as early as 1893 when it noted, "Tucson must have a Sanitarium Hotel, if we would reap the benefit of our health improving climate." Instead, the sick people had to find living arrangements in existing hotels, boardinghouses or, for many, in tents.

As the twentieth century approached, the shortage of tubercular accommodations had become somewhat acute, with the *Star* concluding in 1898, "The knowledge of the existence of a sanitarium here will increase the number of health seekers to the advantage of our business and the spread of its name." One of the initial sanitarium proposals, with possible financial backing by well-known philanthropist Andrew Carnegie, was made in 1902 to have a first-phase facility built for eight hundred patients that later would become "the largest sanitorium in the country." Other possibilities were to build a facility on 40 acres of land a half mile northwest of St. Mary's Hospital or to install up to one hundred cottages, each with three or four bedrooms, on 80 acres of property east of the university. Other options were to build on ground two miles south of the city or on 160 acres in an undisclosed location. None of these plans, however, came to fruition.

What did happen was that next to St. Mary's Hospital, a large, forty-eight-room sanitarium was being constructed in 1899. Designed by Dr. Hiram Fenner, it was described as "a two-story circular structure surrounding an inner patio...to take continuous advantage of the sunshine. It had a shaded porch on the inside and outside circumference of each level. The individual patient rooms opened onto these porches and the doorways were large enough to allow the beds to be wheeled out for those patients who were not ambulatory."

For several reasons, local leaders wanted more than one sanitarium. As the *Star* enthusiastically expounded in 1905 of building sanitariums:

> *Tucson, with her superior climate can...increase the population of the city and the country surrounding her ten times in the next few years, if her citizens will put their shoulders to the wheel and prepare suitable places for those looking for health and happiness.*

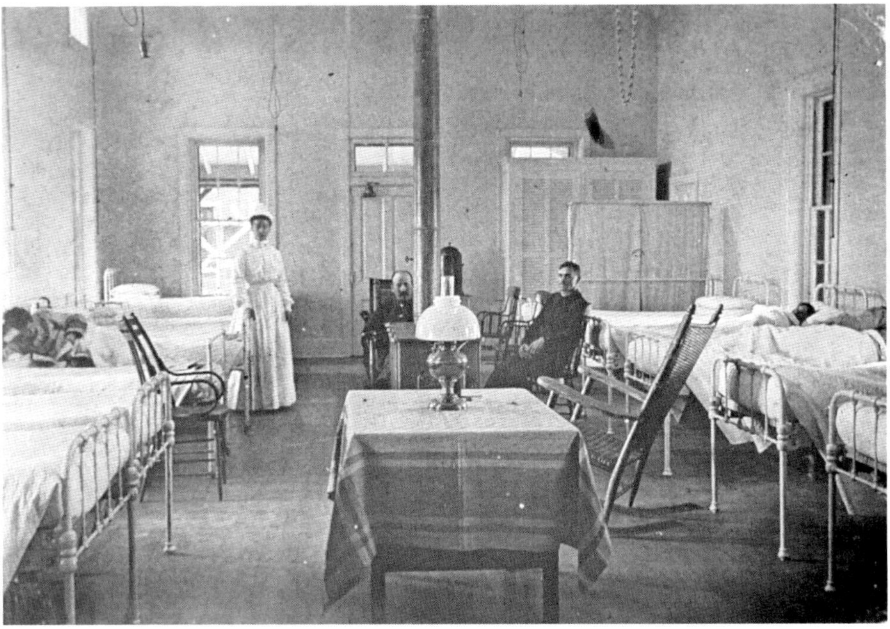

Tuberculosis sanitariums, like this one in New Mexico, circa 1920, were in short supply in Tucson. *U.S. National Library of Medicine.*

Instead of sanitariums being built, what happened was that early in the twentieth century, tents for tuberculosis sufferers began appearing in large numbers on vacant land north of town. They would serve to house the poor or those who couldn't find shelter elsewhere. The *Citizen* reported in 1903 of this area, "Several years ago there were but one or two [tents], and there have multiplied until today about one hundred adorn the mesa. The tents give that part of the city the appearance of a new mining town on a boom."

By 1905, the *Toronto Mail* newspaper described this area, labeled "Tentville," as "just outside the city limits, row upon row of white tents break the monotony of gray sand, mesquite and 'grease' bush....The tents are of cotton or ship canvas with board floors, or 'rammed' earth, or simply rugs laid upon the sand. They are furnished and decorated according to the means and taste of the occupants." The tents cost up to eighty dollars to purchase or could be rented for ten to fifteen dollars per month. Providing supplies were milkmen, butchers, Chinese farmers and others who would circulate daily throughout "Tentville."

A depressing portrayal of the tent city was provided by Dick Hall, who, because of his mother's tuberculosis, moved to Tucson as a boy in 1909. Years later, he estimated that there were several hundred tents and wrote of the place, "The nights were heartbreaking, and as one walked along the dark streets, he heard coughing from every tent. It was truly a place of lost souls and lingering death."

Unable to work, many of these people ran out of money shortly after arriving in town. They thus placed an enormous burden on Tucson charities. As a result, the sick people were scorned by some local residents, and in 1909, one of these people wrote a letter to the *Star* suggesting those with tuberculosis "should be made to live at the foot of the Catalina [M]ountains and not allowed to mingle with the public in the city."

In response to that attitude, Oliver E. Comstock Sr., a printer and itinerant minister who had arrived in town only a few years earlier, "went out to look over the field, and went from tent to tent." That was the beginning of Comstock's long devotion to the ill people of "Tentville," a passion that in 1910 resulted in his creating the Mercy Emergency Hospital, with three tents to serve tubercular patients on Adams Street between Park and Fremont Avenues. This facility would expand over time and eventually became known as the Comstock Hospital.

While the canvas city north of "The Speedway," as the street was then called, was the primary focus of tents, other areas of Tucson were also proposed to contain them. Not surprisingly, this rapid growth of poor people suffering from tuberculosis drew official condemnation in 1907. John P. Hohusen of the Pima County Board of Supervisors complained that a few hundred sick people without financial resources were applying monthly to be cared for at St. Mary's Hospital. Even though the daily county subsidy for each indigent patient was only about two dollars, he said that most of the appeals the board received were denied because granting them would bankrupt the county government. "Indigent patients in the East," Hohusen emphasized, "should be advised through the means of the press and friends who are already here not to come to the Southwest for their health unless they are able to sustain themselves and have the financial means to provide good food and lodging."

The slow transition from Tucson hoping that all health seekers would migrate to town to one that differentiated between rich and poor, moderately ill versus seriously sick, was further spotlighted in 1911 in the *Healthseekers Guide*. It contained a lengthy statement about the community prepared by Herman V. Failor, secretary of the chamber of commerce. In summarizing his comments, the *Star* tried to explain why Tucson's narrative toward tuberculosis sufferers had changed so much over time: "The data [in the guide] tells the plain truth and gives facts which are not encouraging to the indigent invalid, winter prices on commodities being quoted. The booklet [instead] should be the means of bringing to this city many persons of means who seek a better climate."

As Tucson struggled mightily to accommodate poor tuberculosis sufferers, a way to combat the disease was offered in 1910 by the sale of one-cent Red Cross Christmas Seal stamps. With a goal to raise $1 million nationwide, the local campaign was focused on a ten-day event to be held at booths in six downtown retail establishments. Prominent women staffed the tables, and Clotilde Teran Manzo was one of them. Born in Sonora, Mexico, the forty-one-year-old was the wife of Genaro S. Manzo, business associate of Carlos C. Jacome in downtown's Jacome & Manzo dry goods and men's store.

The first day of the sale resulted in almost eighteen thousand stamps being sold. By the end of the effort, close to fifty thousand stamps had been bought, meaning almost $500 was raised. This was more than five times the total sold in Phoenix.

Christmas seals weren't the only anti-tuberculosis effort during the period. "Tuberculosis Day" was originally observed nationwide in 1910, and the following year, it was held on a springtime Sunday. Church ministers were asked to discuss prevention of the disease in their sermons, while "literature was distributed explaining how to best check the ravages" of tuberculosis. In Tucson, almost every place of worship participated.

It wasn't treating tuberculosis sufferers that led to the 1907 opening of Tucson's second full-service hospital. It was, instead, the idea of Blanche B. Whitwell to honor her late husband, physician William S. Whitwell. The couple had lived in both California and New York City, where he ran private sanitariums, and after his death his widow worked with Dr. Hobart Shattuck to construct a wooden, two-story building in Tucson on First Avenue at Adams Street to be known as the Whitwell Hospital.

The hospital had been open less than eighteen months when fire destroyed it completely. Even though she wasn't happy that the Tucson Fire Department sent only its hose wagon and chemical truck to the scene, leaving its fire engine at the downtown station since there were no horses to pull it, Mrs. Whitwell decided to rebuild. As construction of a $50,000 "fireproof" concrete structure was underway, tents were used to house patients.

The "new" Whitwell Hospital had thirty patient rooms, some with en suite bathrooms. There was also an elevator to transport patients. Before the end of 1911, the decision was made to sell the facility, and the new owners changed it to an exclusive tuberculosis facility renamed the Tucson Arizona Sanatorium for Diseases of the Lungs and Throat. The *Star* applauded this

The original Whitwell Hospital burned down in 1908 and was replaced by this "fireproof" structure. *From* Arizona: The Wonderland *by George W. James (1917), Wikimedia Commons.*

transformation, stating that the sanitarium would end a long period of time when "Tucson has lost many wealthy sufferers who would otherwise have come to this city in years past."

By that time, in addition to St. Mary's and Whitwell, Tucson also had Rodgers Hospital downtown. Dr. Mark A. Rodgers, a long-term resident of the city, opened his small institution at the corner of Stone and Ochoa Avenues in 1909. Both births and surgeries were done at the hospital, but "tubercular or other infectious cases" were not admitted.

Although that medical facility was actually built, local hopes for a Southern Pacific Railroad hospital were not to be realized during territorial times. With almost one thousand employees in town and many of the patients of St. Mary's being Southern Pacific workers injured on the job, it seemed reasonable that the company might establish a local hospital. That was the intent in 1902 when Dr. Fenner, then serving as surgeon for the Southern Pacific Company, told a gathering of railroad employees that "the facilities of the present hospital at Tucson [St. Mary's] were inadequate for an emergency." Those at the meeting adopted a resolution calling on the company to construct a local hospital that would exclusively serve railroad employees. But while their arguments may have had merit, Southern Pacific didn't act on them until decades later.

So, by statehood day in 1912, Tucson had two hospitals—St. Mary's and Rodgers—and a few sanitariums. It also had twenty physicians and surgeons, one of whom was a woman. Forty-two-year-old Rosa Goodrich Boido was an 1895 graduate of the prestigious Cooper Medical College in San Francisco, and she worked with her husband, Lorenzo, also a doctor. Their office was on west Pennington Street, and she was listed in the city directory as a "lady physician." In 1903, Boido became Tucson's first licensed physician and several years later led the local effort for women's suffrage in the territory.

With greater medical care, by 1911 people in Tucson were declared to be "enjoying excellent health," according to Dr. Henry E. Crepin, city health officer and bacteriologist. That status had not been obtained simply because of the number of doctors plus the "healthful" climate. Instead, the city as early as 1885 had employed a health officer, and sanitary sewers began being laid in 1900. Then, in 1909, the city government required "that all garbage and rubbish must be kept in a suitable metal can and must be kept covered." The same year, Dr. Crepin began making inspections of "bakeries, meat shops and other places where food stuffs are dispensed." The next year of 1910 saw the Tucson City Council adopt a food storage ordinance, while oil was being sprinkled on pools of water to keep down the mosquito population.

Fifteen years earlier, the *Star* had proudly stated in 1895, "Tucson has the lowest death rate of any place of its population in the United States." Refuting that unsubstantiated publicity claim, the documented death rate in Pima County in 1910 was higher than for any other place in Arizona. Local promoters argued that figure was caused by all the tuberculosis sufferers flocking to Tucson and then dying. In 1908, Dr. Crepin remarkably said of the county's death rate, "[E]liminating the transient consumptives and the peons [poor Mexican Americans], there is practically no death at all in the city."

That statement, like so many others made about the healing qualities of Tucson's climate, was outlandish. There were plenty of local people dying, but the image of the community as a "health resort" had to be maintained by boosters. After all, as Dr. Crepin explained of those the community sought as immigrants, "The greater number of the people whom we are seeking to attract here by our climate are Americans [*sic*] from the east and north."

Chapter 7

SPORT SHORTS

Dr. Henry Crepin wasn't just Tucson's health officer in 1911; he was also a new car owner. To break in the vehicle, he planned a dove hunting trip. When at least three hundred of his friends asked if they could accompany him, the *Arizona Daily Star* indicated Crepin's simple sarcastic reply was, "Certainly."

Hunting had obviously been going on in the region since long before the 1854 Gadsden Purchase, and it continued throughout the territorial period. Quail were shot along the Rillito Creek, and ducks were killed on the Santa Cruz River south of town at Silver Lake. That watery attraction had been created by a man-made earthen dam constructed prior to the Civil War. Built in order to power a flour mill, the dam's lake would also be the site of "a recreation center for boating, swimming, and picnics." A clubhouse along with a one-mile horse racing track were nearby.

Wildlife, including wolves and wildcats for which a monetary bounty was paid by Pima County, was hunted in the mountains around Tucson. Deer were also pursued during a ten-week fall season with a limit of three animals per person. To attract out-of-town hunters, the chamber of commerce in 1911 published a booklet titled "Tucson, a Sportman's Paradise." The *Star* labeled the pamphlet misleading for failing to point out the limited deer hunting season, as well as the illegality of killing mountain sheep and antelope. As for bears, mountain lions, bobcats, coyotes, timber wolves and javelinas, the newspaper editorialized that "there are so few of them that the chance of killing one is far more improbable than otherwise." Even doves,

Deer were hunted during a ten-week fall season around territorial Tucson. *Library of Congress, photo no. 3b40000.*

the newspaper added, "are scarcer than teeth in a chicken." In conclusion, the *Star* wrote, "as a 'Hunter's Paradise,' Tucson is a leg puller."

While hunting may not have been all that great, shooters could improve their skills in town. The Tucson Gun Club held its first tournament in February 1886 in the Santa Cruz River bed, with gunmen aiming at glass balls and live pigeons.

Chickens, on the other hand, were the targets for an 1893 gun club event. "Chickens stood on a box a hundred yards from a man with a gun and laughed at the gun and gunner," the *Arizona Weekly Citizen* dryly commented. Monetary prizes were awarded for the most fatal shots, with dozens of birds not laughing any longer. Another fatal use of fowl was in "chicken pulls." This involved burying a rooster in the ground with only its head showing. A horse rider at full gallop would then try to snatch the bird out of the earth.

Much less lethal was target shooting, sometimes at rocks painted blue. The Tucson Gun Club was initially located at downtown's Elysian Grove amusement area. In early 1909, however, it joined the Blue Rock Gun Club at a range close to Pastime Park, a new recreational facility on Oracle Road a few miles north of the city. The recreational area was opened on New Year's Day 1909 by German immigrant Charles Loebs Sr. Hundreds of trees were planted on several acres of land, and attractions included a beer garden, a picnic area, a tug-of-war pit and other amusements.

One more shooting range, this one three square miles in size, was established by the Tucson Rifle Club in 1910 on federally owned land near the Wilmot train station east of town. Club fees were ten dollars, and sixty people signed up. Members used standard military rifles to shoot at targets on an embankment and were joined on the range by a National Guard unit, along with cadet rifle clubs from the university and Tucson High School.

Back in town, for an 1882 bullfight, a ring with an exclusive viewing area for women was constructed in Levin's Park. In its extensive depiction of the spectacle, the *Citizen* stated that up to 1,400 people, or one-fifth the community's total population, attended. They saw bullfighters in colorful regalia wave red flags in front of bulls with sawed-off horns. The principal bullfighter, Colonel D. Ramón Yanez from Barcelona, Spain, stabbed two spears holding firecrackers into one bull's neck, and the *Citizen* reported, "The exploding crackers drove the bull wild with rage and pain."

Other bullfights would periodically be held, and they were complemented by numerous fights to the death between a variety of other animals. To put a stop to these "sports," in 1895 the Tucson City Council adopted an ordinance outlawing bull, cock and dog fights, and both the *Citizen* and *Star* applauded the ban.

But the law didn't completely stop the bloodletting. At the Orndorff Hotel in 1902, a $500 wager was made on a deadly battle between a pit bull pup and a badger, with the dog killing the wild animal in one minute. Five years later, another dog-badger fight took place with the same result, and the *Citizen* called it "a scene of bloodshed and carnage that was sickening." Tom Marshall, husband of early university educator and influential property developer Louise Foucar Marshall, was one of those in attendance and reportedly made quite a "neat sum" by betting on the dog.

Battles between men also occasionally took place. A few wrestling matches were held, with one of the first being at Levin's Park in 1880. In 1884, there was also a boxing match at the park in front of three hundred spectators. The *Citizen* wrote that it "was the first real prize fight to take place in this city, and it would perhaps be a credit to the city if it should be the last." But in 1893, there was another match with "Australian" Smith defeating "Indian" Smith in five rounds.

The results of a 1910 boxing duel in faraway Reno, Nevada, almost caused bloodshed in Tucson. After African American Jack Johnson defeated James J. Jeffries, "the Great White Hope," European American men across the nation physically took out their frustrations on Black citizens. In Tucson, that meant forty insult-throwing men on both sides of the dispute congregated

Jack Johnson's 1910 Reno, Nevada victory against James Jeffries, "the Great White Hope," caused racial confrontation in Tucson. *Library of Congress, photo no. 31940.*

outside a west Congress Street saloon and had to be separated by a gun-waving deputy sheriff.

While the goal of many athletic endeavors during territorial times was physical punishment, one 1893 event was purely for fun. Accompanied by numerous locals, a California woman supplied with a sack and lantern went nighttime hunting for the elusive snipe. After some time she caught on to the humor concerning the bird and, in response, served her fellow hunters pumpkin pie "with salted water on the side."

While many other sports took place in Tucson, baseball was the primary focus of attention. As early as 1872, a baseball club was being organized, and on the Fourth of July 1879, men living on streets running east–west were playing those from roadways aligned north–south for the city championship.

Those and later teams were usually made up of European American and Mexican American players, but by 1893, a group of African American men had formed their own ball club. They all worked together at the San Xavier Hotel next to the Southern Pacific train station, and the *Star* wrote of them, "There are some clever players among them."

For his part, a Chinese man watching a game in the scorching summer of 1899 wondered aloud how much baseball players were paid. When told "nothing," he replied, "Didn't think American [*sic*] was such big fool to run around so much in hot day for fun. He ought to get no less than five dollars a day for such hard work." To that suggestion, the once racially hostile *Star* replied, "There seems to be both wisdom and good practical sense in the Chinaman's conclusions."

Baseball wasn't limited to local games. All-star teams from town would host or visit other southern Arizona communities, and Tucson went on the road to defeat a Bisbee squad, 20–17, on Christmas Day 1894. Then, in

1907, three hundred fans—many wearing auto caps, white linen dusters and red bandana handkerchiefs—were scheduled to take a special early morning train south of the border to watch the Tucson nine play a club from the mining town of Cananea, Sonora. Before departure, calamity struck. The Tucson team's mascot, a bulldog named "Suspenders," went missing. A posse of almost eighty men quickly formed, and the cherished canine was found. But "Suspenders" and the other fans should have stayed home. In front of three thousand mostly hostile spectators, Cananea prevailed, 22–7, with the visitors committing an astonishing sixteen errors.

Around that time, Tucson's population was approaching twelve thousand people, so there were enough men to form a three- or four-team league, with some players being paid. The games would be organized by the Tucson Baseball Corporation, and Emanuel Drachman was one of the five original directors. In 1903, Drachman purchased the Carrillo's Gardens amusement area, renamed it Elysian Grove and added a baseball diamond. The son of Philip Drachman, a Jewish immigrant from Poland

Tucson's 1893 baseball team, with Emanuel Drachman seated in center. *Arizona Historical Society, #23559-5.*

who arrived in Tucson in 1866, Emanuel was an excellent pitcher as well as an ardent baseball supporter.

By 1906, for unknown reasons, fan interest in Tucson was dwindling rapidly. As the *Citizen* summarized of baseball, "[It's] deader than a jack rabbit hit by a cannon ball." Despite that, when a team from Globe, Arizona, came to town in September 1908, the *Star* made the results of the first game its front-page lead story. Tucson won, 6–1, and thirty-six-year-old Emanuel Drachman pitched. "No one thought Drachman could win, or even could last," the newspaper stated, "but he had the goods and when the nine innings of 'hard luck' were over, Globe was still wondering how he did it."

That victory, however, did not reverse the downward slide in interest. In response, Drachman decided to raise enough money to pay more players a small stipend. Fan interest did pick up enough so that by the spring of 1911, the Armstrong & Company men's clothing store was advertising for as little as $11.90, "a snappy Suit [of wool] to wear" to the opening day's game on May 7.

Baseball was entering its second decade by then at the University of Arizona. Most of the contests in a season of ten games or fewer were played against local clubs or Arizona Territorial Normal School at Tempe (later Arizona State University). Other sports had started to be played on the Tucson campus even earlier, with a basketball game held on a dirt court in 1897. By 1903, Herring Hall, "a small, Roman Revival building constructed of red brick" fronted by four Doric columns, had been built, and it would host both men's and women's basketball games.

Playing its first season at Carrillo's Gardens in 1899, Arizona's football team, with Tom Marshall as one of its fourteen players, lost to Arizona Territorial Normal School by a score of 11–2. In 1900, the team played four games and five in 1901, the year they traveled to Phoenix to battle the eleven from the Phoenix Indian School. "Owing to the bad condition of the [Arizona] football team caused by the milk poisoning," it was later revealed, "the University lost yesterday, 11–0. Six of the football players became sick on milk used in the mess hall."

While generally successful on the gridiron, the Arizona team's 1906 season was canceled for "financial reasons." In each of the next two seasons, the football team played just one game each year. Thus, a 1908 summary of campus athletics prepared by the university concluded, "Football has not been very successful in this institution." But eventually things picked up somewhat.

With football and basketball being played at the university, others in town also took part. By 1893, an effort was being made to put a local football team together, and in 1899, the players held a nighttime practice under the

Women in Tucson were playing basketball by 1900, just like these women, circa 1926. *Library of Congress, photo no. 15577.*

outside lights of the Orndorff Hotel. In 1906, the football squad of the Mexican Athletic Club defeated a team from the Tucson Indian School by a score of 12–5. On the basketball court, after it opened in 1906, Tucson High School had both girls' and boys' teams.

A tennis club was organized in town by 1892, while on campus, according to Terri Dean Riffe's 1986 doctoral dissertation on women's sports at the university, "[s]ix out of the fifteen players in the tennis team picture in a 1907 edition of the *University of Arizona Monthly* were women." The following year, it was reported of the game, "[T]he University has a larger proportion of good [tennis] players than any school in the country."

Occasional track and field meets had included university teams as early as 1897. A decade later, the eight-member men's team traveled to Tempe for a fourteen-event meet and narrowly defeated the Normal School there. Racing contests were also sometimes run at Elysian Grove, with a Labor Day 1909 celebration featuring girls' and boys' sprint races, running of the bases and a relay race.

Another relay race, with twenty men to each side, was run at the San Xavier Mission in 1895. Teams of Native Americans and Mexican Americans faced off, with each man running three hundred yards. The winning team was to receive a small cash prize along with horses and cattle—the Papago team triumphed.

The women of the reservation in 1903 were playing a game somewhat similar to field hockey. "They all had long sticks and kept chasing a small ball," reported the *Citizen*. "The game seemed very laborious, but the women enjoyed it. The game lasted all afternoon."

Even longer in duration was a forty-eight-hour walking contest that took place in 1879, with the actual time walking being around thirty-two hours. There were only two entrants, and the winner covered 124 miles.

Besides billiards shot on tables in saloons, apparently the first official "ball" game played in territorial Tucson was bowling. Leopoldo Carrillo was constructing an alley on Main Street in 1870, and ten years later, a new alley was installed at Levin's Park. A competition that year offered a fifteen-dollar prize to anyone who bowled a perfect score of 300.

On the other hand, golf was a sport that took quite some time to become established in the Tucson desert. In 1906, the *Citizen* stated there were "fine golf links" on country club grounds along "The Speedway" a few miles east of town, but that wasn't exactly the case. The nine-hole dirt course constantly needed to be renovated, and by 1909, the *Star* had noted, "The maintenance of a good golf course in this city, it is believed, will do as much toward attracting the tourist and homeseeker as anything else in an amusement way."

The public response to golf, however, remained underwhelming, and by 1910, the *Citizen* had concluded, "Tucson has an excellent site for a Country Club, but that it is largely in an unimproved state, lacks a club house, and will serve about equally as well for a rifle range or a place for dry-farming experiments." Thus, the newspaper later editorialized, "[a] Country Club is one of the urgent needs of this city. Without it, Tucson can never expect to come into her own as a winter resort."

Plans for a new clubhouse, golf links, tennis courts and rifle range on "The Speedway" were made in 1910 but never implemented. It was four more years before another country club was established, and it would be an eighteen-hole dirt course located east of town on Broadway.

Informal horse racing, for its part, began as early as 1870, and beginning on Christmas Day 1879, a five-day meet was put on at a track south of town. Both one-half-mile and one-mile races were run, and cash prizes up to $200 were awarded. The December races in 1880 took place at the Silver Lake track, and among the horses entered was the unfortunately named "Dud."

With the repeated washing out of the facility at Silver Lake due to flooding of the Santa Cruz River, the need for another horse track emerged. By 1893,

Above: Bowling alleys, like these New York lanes, circa 1900, were available in Tucson by 1870. *Library of Congress, photo no. 62049.*

Right: Many Americans, like Katharine Harley, enjoyed golf before 1912; the game, however, wasn't popular in territorial Tucson. *Library of Congress, photo no. 3b27564.*

plans were made not only for a one-half-mile race course but also a baseball diamond and tennis courts. The new forty-acre recreational facility would be on Twenty-Second Street and Park Avenue and be called Union Park. But it was inconveniently located and would close around 1908.

In 1894, a rodeo was held in town. There were shooting, lassoing and bloodless bullfighting events, but the highlight, according to the *Citizen*, was the bronco riding. One horse not only had never been ridden but also had supposedly killed two men who tried. A ranch cowboy, however, "clung like glue" to the horse and succeeded in riding him.

Downtown, in late 1909, California investors were financing the construction of a greyhound dog track at Elysian Grove. Although the races were promoted, and women sometimes admitted free, the business lasted less than four months. One of the owners concluded, "[T]he real reason for failure lay in the fact that Tucson is not large enough to support the sport."

Lack of attendance wasn't what led to the closure of Elysian Grove in 1911. Instead, it was the anticipated economic and population booms that would result from the arrival of the El Paso & Southwestern Railroad. After eight years of ownership, Emanuel Drachman decided to subdivide the property into residential lots. As a result, the *Citizen* pointed out, "Tucson will be left without an amusement park of its character."

Roller skating lasted much longer. There was a rink at Levin's Park by 1879 that charged twenty-five cents for admission and another two bits to rent skates. A "masquerade" skate was held in 1885, with women getting in at no charge but men having to pay fifty cents. Everyone skating wore a mask, and the *Citizen* reported that "several hundred sightseers were present." Another rink, this one on west Pennington Street, opened in 1887, and its owners promised "[g]ood music, good floor, and good skates."

The subdued sport of swimming went on at an indoor natatorium that opened in 1897 near Main Street. The pool was one hundred feet long by thirty-three feet wide and refilled periodically with 170,000 gallons of water pumped from the nearby Santa Cruz River bed. Women had separate days for swimming, and a few months after opening the *Star* said of the facility that "[it] has already become the center of attraction and enjoyment."

Within fourteen years, however, the building was being called an "old structure," and the city was planning to demolish it in order to widen Alameda Street, while also enlarging a small nearby park. "[W]ith its many happy memories," the *Star* wrote of the swimming pool, "[the natatorium] will soon be a thing of the past, to give place to improvement and more happiness—in a different form."

Chapter 8

NEIGHBORING NEIGHBORHOODS

Along with the natatorium, Tucson's original Chinatown was demolished because of the 1911 urban renewal project. This small residential and commercial district had initially been established in the late 1870s around the intersection of Main and Alameda Streets and, in time, would house up to two hundred men. By the twentieth century, however, the area contained just a few dozen single Chinese men along with some shops and other businesses. These had to be relocated because of the city's street widening and park expansion redevelopment process.

The Chinese men would start anew a few blocks away in Barrio Libre south of Congress Street. About one hundred of their countrymen already resided there along with many Mexican American and European American households. But even that short move by the Chinese was unsuccessfully criticized by more than one hundred Tucsonans in a petition presented to the city council. "The petitioners asserted that although they have no animosity against the Chinese," the *Arizona Daily Star* newspaper reported without irony, "it is generally known that a Chinatown is never desirable as a neighbor, deteriorates the value of adjacent property and renders the immediate vicinity uninhabitable by American [*sic*] families. The council was therefore asked to provide another location more isolated [than Barrio Libre] for the Chinamen."

A similar antagonistic attitude had greeted Chinese men when a few of them first began moving to Tucson around 1875. Within four years, their numbers had reached ten, and the *Arizona Daily Star* in an 1879 article complained, "The Chinese are coming, and with their coming they are bringing their loathsome characteristics."

These men, many of whom were former railroad track workers, settled in an area already containing the homes of some Mexican Americans. They quickly opened a few wash houses, a restaurant and a joss house, a building that "likely provided not only a place for spiritual help (and gambling) but also a focus for business activity, community charities, and celebrations." As dozens more Chinese men arrived, they tended to congregate in this same area, following the time-honored tradition of many immigrants in clustering together in one location for both community and safety.

Around that time, Tucson in 1880 was an almost completely adobe town, with a few distinct but closely aligned neighborhoods. There was Barrio Libre, Chinatown and residences and a church built on the original presidio site. East of Stone Avenue, surrounding the former Military Plaza as well as near the new railroad depot, some dispersed homes were being constructed primarily for European American families.

The March 1880 arrival of the railroad not only helped more than double the town's 1870 population of 3,215 within a decade to 7,007, but it also supplied fired bricks and lumber for construction. This change launched a relentless and ongoing print-media attack on the use of adobe. "[T]he day is not far distant," the *Arizona Weekly Citizen* predicted in October 1879, "when the adobe will be referred to as a relic of barbarism."

The *Citizen* and *Star* mocked using adobe bricks for construction once the railroad's 1880 arrival made lumber available. *Library of Congress, photo no. 008178.*

With further population growth anticipated following the railroad's arrival, the need for additional housing was forecast. Simultaneously, some leading citizens began constructing large, imposing homes. Merchant William W. Williams was one of those with the enormous residence in which he would host President Rutherford B. Hayes. Leopoldo Carrillo was also included among those making substantial improvements to their homes even as *El Fronterizo* newspaper pointed out that Carrillo in 1881 owned 70 of the community's 2,200 total houses.

Tucson's seemingly bright prospects led the *Arizona Weekly Star* to proclaim in 1883 that "a new era of prosperity is dawning upon our city." That forecast proved to be wishful thinking. A Tucson bank failed following the downturn of the Tombstone mining industry in the early 1880s, and the railroad didn't turn out to be the economic engine that was anticipated. As a result, territorial Tucson entered a long-term period of population and business decline. One of the initial casualties was Estevan Ochoa, whose freighting business quickly fell into bankruptcy, forcing his family in 1884 to leave their palatial home on Stone Avenue for more modest accommodations on Meyer Street. By 1885, amusement park owner Alex Levin had lost his home on Stone Avenue to foreclosure, and it was sold by the sheriff for $5,200.

With the city's population actually decreasing, some homes in Barrio Libre were abandoned and used as garbage dumps. Also in the barrio near Meyer Street was what the *Star* in 1893 disparagingly called "a little collection of battered pieces of oil cans. Often of nights, particularly dark nights, this miniature tin hut may be seen all alight within.... The place is the scene of the murder of a Mexican many years ago." Eventually, this collection of various odds and ends that first appeared around 1870 would become treasured to Tucsonans as *El Tiradito*, the Wishing Shrine.

Only a few blocks away in the early 1890s, north Main Street was being called "the most attractive thoroughfare in the city." These luxury homes were often built of brick, stone or, in some cases, locally quarried volcanic rock, materials that the *Star* fully endorsed. "The time has come," the newspaper expounded in 1891, "to discard mud [adobe] houses and to adopt the modern style, and this must be done if Tucson would receive that attention she is entitled to." Following such advice, wagon maker Fred Ronstadt, who was married to Sara Levin, Alex Levin's daughter, was having a four-room brick house built near the abandoned Military Plaza in 1893. Elsewhere, however, adobe bricks continued to be used extensively.

Tucson's economic doldrums were beginning to fade by the late 1890s, with both population growth and new home construction picking up. On

Main Street, the original Owl's Club, a brick bachelor pad for four men, was built in 1899, and by 1908 retailer Albert Steinfeld had purchased the property referred to as "the showplace of Tucson." A few blocks away at Stone Avenue and Pennington Street, Dr. Hiram Fenner was moving into a new $9,000 home in 1897, reportedly the most expensive house built until then. These "modern" homes were presumably outfitted with a water closet (i.e., indoor plumbing), an advancement that had finally reached Tucson.

As homes were built in late nineteenth-century Tucson and sanitary sewers installed, indoor plumbing became more common. *Library of Congress, photo no. 102127.*

While land south of the railroad line was the focus of most new home construction at the end of the nineteenth century, some residential development was occurring on the other side of the tracks. One of those homes was that of postmaster and lumber yard owner J. Knox Corbett. In 1898, he moved his family into a six-room frame residence on north Sixth Avenue. A few blocks west, after being widowed and remarried, Fred Ronstadt in 1904 had an imposing house built on Sixth Avenue and Fifth Street. Even farther from the center of town, residential development was occurring around the University of Arizona. It was promotionally, and unbelievably, stated by the *Star* of this location that "[i]t is always from four to ten degrees cooler in summer than down in the city. In the winter, it is from five to ten degrees warmer on account of the warmth reflected from the south side of the Santa Catalinas"—mountains that were at least eight miles away.

With Tucson's growing population having surpassed 7,500 by the end of the nineteenth century, both local newspapers were declaring that good times had returned. "There are more residences being constructed and contracted for," the *Star* gleefully announced in September 1899, "than at any time in the history of Tucson."

By then, some of the community's neighborhoods were heading toward becoming mostly segregated settlements. As Thomas Sheridan wrote in *Los Tucsonenses*, the development around the Military Plaza was "an overwhelmingly Anglo neighborhood," with almost 90 percent of the 307 households residing in the area in 1897 being European American.

In addition to the predominately Mexican American Barrio Libre south of downtown, Barrio Tonto, later Anita, developed north of the railroad tracks and west of Main Street as another Mexican American residential district. Eventually, Yaqui immigrants fleeing Mexico would also move into these two areas. But most new housing development was focused at European Americans because Tucson's racial character was shifting. In 1880, nearly two-thirds of the city's 7,007 residents had been Mexican Americans. Because of decreased immigration from Mexico, along with the departure of some blue-collar jobs from Tucson, by 1900 that percentage had shrunk to 55 percent; it would continue to decline in the early years of the twentieth century.

Thus, Tucson was growing in population while transforming into a majority European American community for the first time. Mirroring that early twentieth-century change, the variety of religious institutions was expanding significantly as the number of Protestants increased. Following the 1859 plans for a new Catholic church on the central plaza to provide religious services to the mostly Mexican American community, it was about two decades before other Christian denominations established a local presence. By 1879, a Protestant church had been built on land where the presidio once stood, a religious structure that was soon occupied by Congregationalists. Presbyterians were meeting on north Stone Avenue, while Methodist-Episcopalians were holding services at Stone and Pennington. In 1882, a Baptist church was completed at Stone and Eighth Street, and Grace Episcopal Church would be consecrated in April 1893 at Stone and Broadway. A few years after that, a new, larger Catholic cathedral opened on south Stone Avenue.

While some small Protestant congregations initially held services in homes or other limited spaces early in the twentieth century, with support from Presbyterians, in 1905 a Papago mission congregation began meeting in a building on Twenty-Fourth Street south of Barrio Libre. The following year, a new $21,000 Methodist church opened on Sixth Avenue near Twelfth Street in a structure called "the finest church edifice in the entire Territory with the exception of the Catholic Cathedral here." In 1908, a new Presbyterian church costing more than $20,000 was finished at Scott and Ochoa, and a new Baptist church was also opened. Fundraising began in 1906 to build a Jewish synagogue, with local women contributing $1,000. By 1910, the "handsome and modern structure" on south Stone Avenue was completed

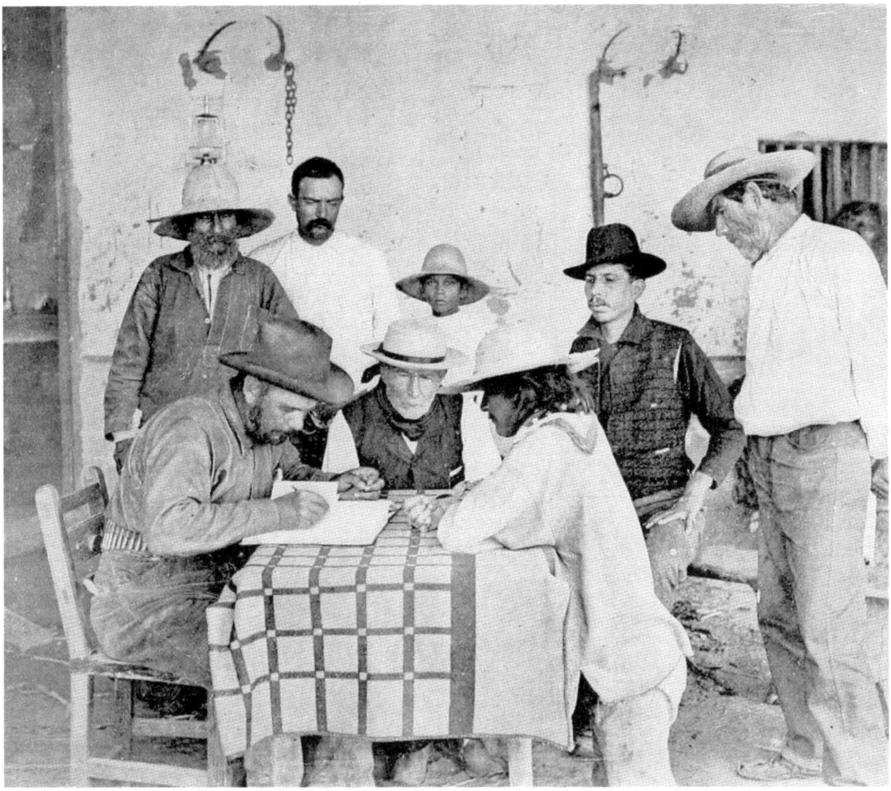

Territorial Tucson's population was a diverse mix of people, as shown in this 1895 photo. *Smithsonian Institution, Bureau of American Ethnology, Wikimedia Commons.*

at a cost of $4,700, becoming the first synagogue in the territory. In 1911, the twenty-five members of the Christian Church decided to erect a small building out by the University of Arizona at Second Avenue and Fifth Street. Also that year, there was a Baptist Mexican Mission on south Meyer in Barrio Libre, but its members were facing harassment. "Frequent complaint has been made by Rev. [Oliver] Comstock to the police department," the *Citizen* reported, "concerning the attempts to break up the protestant meetings by irresponsible Mexicans." Other religious facilities included Lutherans holding services in a civic club hall and Christian Scientists meeting on Pennington Street.

One other congregation was in Tucson by 1911. To serve a Black community of about 220 people, many of whom lived in the vicinity, an African Methodist church was holding services at Seventeenth Street and Convent in Barrio Libre.

A modern photograph of the Prince Chapel African Methodist Episcopal Church building, constructed in 1912. *Library of Congress, photo no. az0106.*

The growth in Protestant churches in Tucson in the first years of the twentieth century reflected the shift to a European American majority population, the increase in the total number of people in town and the subsequent need for additional housing. To oversee this residential construction, the city created the position of building inspector in 1903. But the new housing supply couldn't keep pace with demand, and by 1904, the *Citizen* was claiming that Tucson had a "house famine" that would have dire consequences. "No houses, no tourists," the newspaper moaned, "no tourists, dull business, is about the way to sum the matter up."

Around that time, Pueblo Legarra had moved his family into the historic Cordova house on north Meyer Street. Called by the *Citizen* "the richest Indian in the Papago tribe," Legarra was said to own "several hundred horses and cattle and is comfortably fixed. He is regarded as one of the shrewdest business men among the Indians."

Back on nearby north Main Street, J. Knox Corbett in 1907 was completing yet another, even larger new house for his family at an estimated cost of $15,000. Other new homes would soon be built on the street, including a $35,000 brick and lumber structure by Eliza Ward Rockwell, the widow of a Milwaukee industrialist. Much more modestly, Gertrude McLeary Ochoa, the widowed daughter-in-law of the deceased Estevan

Ochoa, had a $4,000 brick home built in 1908 near her parents' house at Main Street north of Franklin.

Many other homes priced between $2,500 and $5,000 were also being built in developing subdivisions all around the bustling community. But construction continued to not keep pace with demand, so early in 1907 the *Citizen* amazingly declared, "Tucson is growing too rapidly."

To supply even more housing, on the west side of town near the Santa Cruz River, there was construction by the Riverside Land and Development Company. On St. Mary's Road was El Rio subdivision, where no house costing less than $2,000 nor tent houses would be permitted. East of Stone Avenue and south of "The Speedway" was the City of Tucson subdivision. Closer to the University of Arizona campus was University Heights, which contained three dozen vacant blocks ready for home building. South of Twenty-Second Street and east of Seventh Avenue in the Southern Heights Addition were 350 vacant lots selling for between $125 and $400. East of downtown on either side of the railroad tracks were three subdivisions: Altadena, Bruckner's and Manlove. Their developers unashamedly declared to potential customers: "Buy real estate, young man. No matter where you buy. It will prove a good investment, but BUY!!!"

It wasn't only single-family homes being built. Near the former Military Plaza, numerous apartment houses were constructed between 1880 and 1909. Farther north, in 1908, the $30,000 Rincon Apartment building with central heating was completed at Sixth Avenue and Third Street.

Men weren't the only ones developing new housing. Both Louise Foucar Marshall, the first woman instructor at the University of Arizona starting in 1899, and Marian C. Stanley, an assistant professor of philosophy later at the university, were investing in residential development.

All this new home construction still couldn't keep pace with demand, as the local economy was booming. Mines were doing well, the Southern Pacific Railroad employed more than one thousand men and the tourism- and health-related industries were expanding. As a result, by 1910, Herman Failor of the chamber of commerce was stating, "We need houses renting for between $20 and $30 per month....We must have more houses or our tourists will swamp us and then go away angry and knock the city, because they could find no place to stay."

That may have been the case, but the *Star* in 1910 declared that "the town has the air of prosperity and success." Around the same time, the *Citizen* surprisingly changed its stance on the use of adobe. It editorialized that compared to fired brick, an adobe home "is cooler in summer, warmer in winter [and] better suited to the climate in every way." The newspaper thus reversed decades of belittlement and declared adobe "the ideal" building material. The *Star*, on the other hand, was promoting as "eminently suited to this climate" fired brick or frame California Mission–style homes, the construction method largely used north of the railroad tracks to build new houses.

Those types of homes were also found along north Main Street. To make room for even more luxury housing in the center of town, additional vacant land was needed. As a result, Dr. Fenner, a major property owner by then in Chinatown, when notified in March 1910 of health problems in the area, "promised [the city council] to cause the immediate removal of the tenants of the property."

Pressure to level Chinatown soon led to an early obituary in the *Star*. "The Chinese quarters in the northwest end of town are doomed," proclaimed the newspaper in April 1910. It described that the buildings in the general vicinity were "for the most part are old and antiquated, and it is said to be the purpose of those most interested to replace these buildings with more modern ones, making that section of the city one of the neatest in Tucson."

A demolition contractor was hired in early January 1911, and within a few days, some of the buildings of the area were rubble. Much of the vacant land,

Luxury homes were built along north Main Street and in surrounding areas starting in the 1890s. *From* Arizona: The Wonderland *by George W. James (1917), Wikimedia Commons.*

however, would sit idle for years. Despite the demand for additional luxury housing, it wouldn't be until 1915 that a new Tucson's Woman's Club opened on part of the original Chinatown. Among other buildings eventually to be constructed on the redeveloped site would be Fairchild Court, a ten-unit, single-story apartment housing complex. New single-family housing may have been in huge demand, but Tucson's original Chinatown redeveloped site wouldn't play much of a role in meeting that need.

Chapter 9

COMMERCIAL CENTERS

Almost a quarter century before Chinatown and the natatorium were demolished in 1911, Chinese-owned businesses had been under assault. The Fashion Restaurant in 1885 displayed a poster reading, "The Chinese Must Go," while advertising that it was a place "where only white cooks and waiters are employed." The *Arizona Daily Star* naturally endorsed those efforts. "The fact that the Fashion keeps white cooks, white waiters and employees goes to show that it patronizes home labor; hence, it ought to receive the patronage of all," the newspaper stressed.

Complaining about business competition certainly wasn't done earlier in Tucson. In 1855, Mark Aldrich reportedly became the first "American" merchant in town. Six years later, he spearheaded local support for the Confederacy. The *Weekly Arizonian* newspaper stated there were only eight merchants in Tucson a few years after the Civil War ended, but it noted with pride that this number had grown considerably by 1870. The community by then had several grocery and drugstores along with some pawn shops, but wholesaling and retailing in the tiny town remained difficult, with Apache attacks occasionally keeping supplies from reaching the settlement.

German native Albert Steinfeld had taken a six-day stagecoach trip from San Diego to arrive in town in 1872 to work for the Zeckendorfs commercial firm. He wasn't impressed with what he found. "There were no telegraph lines, no lights except candles, which we had to make mostly ourselves, and no way of reaching people except by word of mouth," Steinfeld recalled

The American Indian Wars ended in 1886; raids by Apache warriors were no longer a threat to commercial freight haulers. *Library of Congress, photo no. 34278.*

many years later. As for needed merchandise in the remote community, Steinfeld explained:

> *Our supplies came from San Francisco on the west once a month by boat through the mouth of the Colorado River, and from there were* [wagon] *teamed to Tucson, taking from 60 to 90 days from San Francisco. The supplies we got from eastern points were shipped to the end of the Santa Fe railroad in Kansas, and from there by mule or ox team, and took from four to six months time.*

Overcoming the problems of distance and disruption, the town's first commercial center developed along Main Street. The businesses there included the Tully & Ochoa freight company store along with retailers Lord & Williams and Zeckendorfs. By 1880, with the easy transportation of goods provided by the railroad focused around the Toole Avenue depot site, some businesses had turned the corner of Main Street and were heading eastward along Congress Street. These included the Hudson & Company Bank, the

Congress Hall Saloon and the U.S. Post Office. Other stores were scattered throughout Barrio Libre south of Congress Street. Back on Main Street, both Lord & Williams and Zeckendorfs had new 1,600-square-foot showrooms built in 1879. From the Lord & Williams store, mining equipment, groceries, liquor, clothing, cigars and many other goods were available.

Because they often had access to investment capital, it was mostly "American" men who operated the major businesses in town. There were some exceptions, of course, and it wasn't only men who were merchants, either. Around 1880, advertisements for businesses operated by women were frequent in both the *Citizen* and the *Star*. A native of France, Marie Ange Merrill was a dressmaker with a store near the Catholic church, while Ella O'Keefe had a millinery business on north Meyer Street. Mrs. Webb originally had a coffee shop but then opened a wine and beer hall. With the railroad about to arrive in March 1880, Mrs. S.M. Gillett established the People's Store on Congress Street at Stone Avenue, selling groceries. Meanwhile, Mrs. Hutton had opened a beauty parlor for women, but she also advertised "Gentlemen's mustaches and wigs made to order." By the summer of 1880, Mrs. M.J. Smith had changed occupations; she closed her hat shop and bought the Delmonico Restaurant from early entrepreneur Nellie Cashman.

With business booming at the end of 1880, it was reported there were forty-three retail liquor stores in Tucson as well as twenty-three saloons. Besides drinking, the town's seven thousand residents could choose from twenty-three restaurants, fifteen grocery stores, two banks and twelve dry goods stores. There were also thirty-one *tendajons*, or small Mexican-owned shops, with many of them in Barrio Libre, and a few Chinese-owned stores had been established. Visitors to town had two hotels and eight lodging houses to choose from for places to stay.

While commercial prospects were generally bright after the railroad's arrival, one business controversy quickly surfaced. Mexican coinage, or "adobe dollars" in local parlance, had been accepted in Tucson stores since the Gadsden Purchase. That was only reasonable since much of Tucson's business came from south of the border. While the exchange rate could vary slightly, in 1880 many Tucson businessmen decided to impose a flat 10 percent surcharge on the use of Mexican coinage. That decision was blasted by the *Star*, which called it "a stupidity unparalleled in commercial history." The surcharge, however, did not entirely halt the use of Mexican coins, but their value did fall over time so that by 1901 "adobe dollars" were worth only half their face value.

It wasn't accepting Mexican coinage that led to the decline of Tucson business fortunes after 1880. Instead, it was a slowly sinking economic downturn caused by numerous factors, which meant that a number of longtime businesses would close, including Lord & Williams in 1881 and both the Hudson & Company Bank and the Tully & Ochoa freighting firm in 1884. The next year, due to financial difficulties, Levin's Park changed ownership, and Alex Levin would then try his hand at operating several saloons. By 1887, however, he was reportedly living in Mexico City.

In 1882, the faltering economy didn't deter young businessman Albert Steinfeld from becoming the chief selling agent for Zeckendorfs. Also by 1882, there were some significant changes in Tucson's commercial landscape. Five hotels were open, including the Cosmopolitan on Main Street, later renamed the Orndorff, and there were six "American," four Mexican and nine Chinese restaurants. Additionally, the number of saloons remained high, with one being the Bon Ton on Meyer Street. Operated by Mrs. R.P. Wilbur and her husband, it was written that she "presides at the bar and is an accomplished mixiologist." Women tending bar wouldn't be tolerated forever in territorial Tucson. Trying to combat prostitution, in 1899 the city council adopted an ordinance doing "away with all women and girls employed in and about the saloons."

Even though the *Citizen* in 1884 had declared that Tucson was "the commercial metropolis of the Territory and it will never lose its prestige," economic prospects continued to dim throughout the 1880s. That didn't stop Mariano Samaniego from advertising in 1885 for his saddle shop on south Meyer Street: "I want all my friends to patronize me and those who are not my friends I want to make them so." That same year, a party of Black citizens named Hill took over the Grand Central restaurant, and the *Citizen* wrote, "They intend making it a first-class restaurant in every respect." Also opening in 1885 was the Legal Tender, a saloon on west Congress Street. Not only did Louis Neri, the proprietor, promise to keep "the best of wines and liquors always on hand," but he also made home deliveries.

By early 1887, the Chinese-hating Fashion Restaurant was closed, replaced by the Saddle Rock Oyster House. Eating fresh oysters had become a craze as soon as they became available with the railroad's arrival. In 1882, a dozen "Fresh, Eastern" oysters could be purchased for seventy-five cents, and the Maison Doree restaurant in 1885 offered not only oysters but also fresh frogs.

To keep food like that from spoiling, reliable refrigeration would come in handy, and by 1892 electricity was being introduced. A generator was

"Old Main," the University of Arizona's original building, was Tucson's first to have electric lights. *Library of Congress, photo no. HABS ARIZ, 10-TUCSO, 14A-3.*

obtained by the University of Arizona, and in July it was lighting about fifty bulbs in Old Main, the only building on campus. A few months later, local leaders, including Dr. Hiram Fenner and Louis C. Hughes of the *Star*, saw for themselves the lights in Old Main being turned on. Shortly after that, an electricity generating plant for the entire community was under construction. The evolution from candles to oil lamp to electric light had been gradual, but in a steaming July 1898, it was approvingly noted by the *Citizen*, "Last year there were six electric fans in use in Tucson. Thus far this year no less than 55 have been put in and before the hot weather is over, probably half as many more will be in motion and the terror of the hottest day are done away with."

Around that same time, the local business climate was still in the dumps. "Things cannot be worse than they are now," concluded the *Citizen* in late 1892, but business-minded women and men kept trying. The new Rotieserie Parisienne restaurant, managed by Madam A. Touquet, offered "Regular French dinner—50¢." In 1894, J. Knox Corbett established a lumber yard on Sixth Avenue north of the railroad tracks, becoming one of the first merchants to occupy that virgin commercial territory. That same year, the *Citizen* characterized a portion of Tucson business as "[a]ll the small meat markets are kept by Mexicans, the small groceries by Chinamen, and the small saloons generally by foreign nationalities." The article didn't mention the ethnicity of who ran the city's restaurants, but by 1898 it was observed, "There are fifteen restaurants in Tucson, besides hotel dining rooms, private boarding houses, chili con carne establishments, the open air joints, and the customary hot, noon, lunch-only places. You cannot starve in the old pueblo, while you have dinero."

With an economic upswing finally underway by the late 1890s, commercial development remained focused on Congress Street, while retailers and others continued their slow but inevitable push toward the railroad depot. This expansion also meant that there would be calls to demolish "The Wedge," a peninsula-shaped part of Congress Street just blocks west of Stone Avenue. Eventually, all these buildings would be removed, opening the area for new development.

Even as large commercial structures began appearing in Tucson early in the twentieth century, including the five-story Santa Rita Hotel, movies began being shown outdoors at Emanuel Drachman's Elysian Grove recreational area. The film *Fairy Land* was advertised in April 1904 as being "over 900 feet long," and it was followed a few months later by *The Great Train Robbery*. Films could also be seen indoors at the Opera House on Congress Street, where in April 1904 "over a mile of moving pictures run through, with battle scenes and wrestling matches up to date....Admission only 25 and 35 cents."

Opened in 1903, the Santa Rita Hotel was among several tall buildings once dominating Tucson's downtown skyline. *Postcard collection, 1904, Wikimedia Commons.*

While movies provided family entertainment, it was reported in 1902 that there were still forty-four saloons in Tucson, or one for about every two hundred people. In 1898, open gambling was also done at five establishments, but a crackdown during the following decade resulted in many forms of gambling being outlawed both in the city and across the territory. That didn't stop the betting, of course, and in early 1906 a fixed game of poker at the Legal Tender saloon received extensive coverage by the *Citizen*.

Following its semi-successful crusade against gambling, the Democratic-controlled Tucson City Council went after saloons. In early 1906, it limited the number to thirty, even though there were considerably more in existence. The council also drastically increased the annual saloon fee from $140 to $600, while revoking one saloon's license because of the "vile language" being used there.

Tucson's saloonkeepers naturally weren't going to remain silent about these assaults. They formed a group that in March 1906 decided to oppose a proposed $200,000 city bond program to "extend and improve the [city's] water service and the fire department." To promote its arguments, the saloon league published a pamphlet that stated, "The City of Tucson has now sufficient revenue from various sources to enable it to make improvements gradually, without resorting to any new obligations to be imposed upon our posterity....Vote against the bonds. Repudiate the City Council."

On election morning, March 29, 1906, the *Citizen* declared, "It is doubtful if Tucson has ever before known so exciting an election." Lined up near the one polling station in town, carriages carried banners that read, "Vote Against the Bonds." For their part, before the voting even began, bond supporters "were out getting matters lined up for the day." Once balloting started, charges were filed that the saloonkeepers were buying votes by agreeing to pay the mandatory $2.50 voting fee, or poll tax, for men opposing the bonds.

A total of 525 votes were cast, with those in favor accounting for 322. But because a two-thirds majority was needed for passage, the bond measure failed. "The elements in opposition," the *Citizen* editorialized, "were the lower strata of the community" that included saloonkeepers, socialists and non-progressives "who hate bathtubs and sewers."

In the December 1906 city elections, pro-saloon Republicans wrested control of the council from the Democrats. Before they left office, however, the Democrats raised the annual saloon fee from $600 to $1,000. Wanting to pass the water service and fire improvements bonds, the new Republican council promised to revoke the license increase. The bond question was then

Fred Ronstadt's business was constantly innovating. It sold wagons and then automobiles, while placing ads in city directories and publishing a catalogue. *From the 1902 Tucson City Directory.*

placed back on the ballot in March 1907, and this time the measure passed overwhelmingly. A few weeks later, the saloon fee was returned to $600.

Despite all the political controversy, the local economy was humming. "Business with us during the past year [1906] has been excellent," stated Fred Ronstadt. Retailer Albert Steinfeld echoed those sentiments by saying, "We have enjoyed an excellent year's business and it has eclipsed that of last year." In March 1906, a few years after buying out Zeckendorfs, Steinfeld opened a new department store on Stone Avenue at Pennington Street. Tucson's retail core was thus expanding from just being along Congress Street; it was also spreading out around the intersection of Congress with Stone Avenue.

Simultaneously, the warehouses these growing businesses depended on to store their merchandise after it arrived by rail were expanding along Toole Avenue west of the depot. With the railroad's 1880 appearance, a few businesses, including Zeckendorfs, had small warehouses built near the train station. By 1910, larger structures stretched all the way to the west side of Stone Avenue, where both Steinfeld's and the Southern Pacific Company had enormous storage buildings.

As that expansion happened, Tucson's small Chinese community was taking over much of the daily retail needs business. In 1907, there were almost fifty Chinese-owned general merchandise stores, and by 1911 the *Star* concluded, "Formerly, Tucson had from twenty to thirty little *tendajons*, or places where groceries were kept for sale by Mexicans. Today there is not one of the kind in Tucson. The Chinaman, with his more economical way and closer profit, not only forced them to the wall, but over it."

Dozens of Chinese groceries were scattered throughout territorial Tucson. *Arizona Historical Society, MS 1242.*

Another group of immigrants was selling various things by early 1907. A man identified as Syrian had a fruit stand on Congress Street, and within a few months, Syrians were offering Mexican silks and other goods from south of the border. By the spring of 1908, another Syrian, thirty-two-year-old James Etule, had opened a barbershop on Congress Street.

While Tucson's business opportunities kept growing early in the twentieth century, there were some problems. The community's cost of living was high, with groceries being especially expensive. In response, in 1909 more than 150 households began ordering groceries to be delivered by rail from either Los Angeles or Kansas City. Another innovation in retailing appeared in 1911, when Fred Ronstadt's company printed a fifty-page catalogue of Arizona-produced goods, becoming the first firm to do so in the territory.

One more first occurred in February 1910, when a biplane used a temporary landing strip at Elysian Grove to entertain local enthusiasts. To commemorate the occasion, the Steinfeld Department Store had a display in its show windows exhibiting a brightly colored plane "carrying out in miniature the details of one famous [flight] pattern of the modern sky flyer."

The advent of aviation in Tucson only temporarily stole the headlines from the on-again, off-again drive against saloons. In 1911, there was a successful campaign to prohibit a saloon from being established on east Congress Street. Simultaneously, the license of the Double Stamp saloon on west Congress Street was revoked because the place had a machine that showed "lewd and obscene pictures." In 1914, all saloons would be put out of business when the newest state in the Union adopted prohibition.

Despite the distractions of saloons and other vices, Tucson commercial prospects were bright with the approach of statehood in February 1912. As the *Citizen* had proclaimed a few months earlier, "A healthy tone of optimism pervades the business district. Statehood, railroads, smelter, new mines opening up and the promise of a banner cattle year, are the indices which Tucsonians declare point toward unparalleled business welfare."

Chapter 10

A TOE TICKLER AND OTHER TUCSONANS

EARNING A LIVING

With a thriving Tucson economy in the first years of the twentieth century, a 1912 *Citizen* editorial titled "Women in Business" pointed out a popular view on the subject: "Women are not supposed to be temperamentally suited to the transaction of business on a complicated scale." The paper then indicated that it did not agree with that suggestion.

The belief that women couldn't manage a business certainly hadn't been adhered to in Tucson since at least the late 1870s, when Nellie Cashman opened a dining establishment. By 1912, the city directory listed twenty-four cafés and restaurants—four of those were operated by Mexican American women in the first two blocks of south Meyer Street. Native of Mexico Dolores Salazar was a laundress before becoming the proprietor of the Mexicano Restaurant, while Carmen Romez de Terán ran the nearby Sonorense Restaurant. The Star Restaurant was operated by Francisca Delahanty, who had emigrated from Mexico in 1897, and the interestingly named Togo Restaurant was run by Dolores Grijalva.

Within a few months, those four establishments on south Meyer were joined by another restaurant operated by a Mexican American woman. La Mexican opened on St. Patrick's Day 1912 under the watchful eye of fifty-two-year-old Maria Gomallanes. The *Citizen* declared her "one of the best cooks in the city." She served tamales and enchiladas made to order

South Meyer Street in 1912 contained several restaurants operated by Mexican American women. *Arizona Historical Society, #42014.*

while meals for a week could be purchased for $2.50. Maria, along with the others running dining establishments on south Meyer, certainly showed that women were obviously "temperamentally suited to the transaction of business on a complicated scale."

STANDING UP

Since first arriving in Tucson in the 1870s, the Chinese were the focus of many racial taunts. Following the end of the American Indian Wars in 1886, Native Americans, Mexican Americans and African Americans had been discriminated against by European Americans, but it was the Chinese that seemed to get the worst of it.

In the early years of the twentieth century, that unenviable position apparently began to shift. As they gained greater economic prosperity, Tucson's few hundred Chinese residents seemed to obtain enhanced social status. Simultaneously, Tucson's and Arizona's small African American communities got more discriminatory attention, culminating in a 1909 territorial law that allowed school districts to establish segregated schools. Tucson's school district, however, did not send its forty or so African American students to a separate school until it became legally mandated following statehood.

In 1910, wanting to be referred to as a "colored man," W.B. Bush had vociferously objected when Texas native James Graham directed a derogatory racial slur at him instead. Bush and Graham were both employed by the prestigious Old Pueblo Club. Upon its 1908 opening in a new, three-story building on south Stone Avenue, the *Star* declared that the club "will become the center for the gathering of the businessmen and public-spirited citizens generally in a friendly spirit."

Bush and Graham were certainly not friendly toward each other one day in April 1910. They began arguing about something, with Graham eventually calling Bush a "nigger." According to the *Star*, "Bush [said] he courteously informed the white man that not having been reared in the south, he objected to the term." Ignoring Bush, Graham used the offensive word again, and Bush then "rolled off a few choice epithets of his own."

The two men were soon arrested, Bush ironically for using "abusive language" and Graham for being drunk and disorderly. The following day, both were fined fifteen dollars by Police Judge W.J. Lindenfeld. Bush was able to pay the fine, but Graham couldn't, so was sent to jail for fifteen days.

An Independent Life

Employed while in her thirties as Tucson's first librarian, Nellie Pomroy served in the position from 1887 to 1896. The library was located on the second floor of city hall on Court Street and, along with a small selection of books, offered "popular magazines and papers of the day." A January 1889 story in *El Fronterizo* outlined library activities, while a June 1890 *Citizen* article stated that more than two hundred patrons had used the library the previous month and almost four hundred books had been checked out.

By 1890, Nellie Pomroy was also a public school teacher. Ten years later, she is shown, along with eight other women and five men, in front of a school building for a group photo.

Nellie was still teaching in 1902, but she eventually retired and devoted herself to civic duties and social gatherings. Having never married, in

Nellie Pomroy, no. 13, shown with other school teachers around 1900. *Arizona Historical Society, #3093.*

addition to being involved with a bridge club, she entertained other women at her home at the corner of Alameda and Court Streets. She was also on the board of directors of the Children's Home Society and was a very active member of Grace Episcopal Church. She served as president of the church guild in 1905 and left $5,000 to the church in her will.

Besides her house, Nellie owned a small commercial lot and building on east Congress Street. In 1904, she took her tenant Mr. Berry to court because he was trying to profit by selling off improvements that had been made to the building, and she eventually prevailed.

Nellie decided to sell the business property in 1911 and got a record price for it. Sold for $15,000, or $600 per front foot for the twenty-five-foot-wide lot that was fifty-seven feet deep, the *Citizen* proclaimed the sale "the highest price ever paid for realty in any city of Arizona."

While she could work and own property in 1911, Nellie Pomroy couldn't vote. That began to change the following year when Arizona's male voters supported women's suffrage. Once Tucson women started registering to vote in the spring of 1913, she was one of the earliest to add her name to the list. Nellie Pomroy gave her occupation then as "retired librarian" and her age simply as "over 21."

Honesty as a Policy

Pablo Lijero, a member of the Papago tribe, lived in the mountains about eighty miles west of Tucson. Whether he had personally experienced racial animosity is unknown, but it certainly was common for members of his tribe and other Native Americans. In 1859, the *Weekly Arizonian* wrote, "[T]he [American Indian] man is, perhaps, the laziest, most worthless and despicable of the human family."

At least in 1883 for a few weeks, thirty-two-year-old Pablo Lijero helped change that negative perception of his people. He found a stray horse and turned the animal over to an "American," expecting that the animal's owner would reclaim it. But after two weeks that still hadn't happened, so Pablo retrieved the horse and took it all the way into Tucson. He gave it to a Catholic priest, who followed the legal steps necessary to track down the owner.

"The honesty of the Papago," exclaimed the *Citizen* in response to Pablo's actions, "would have been commendable in a white man, certainly it is more so in an Indian, at whose door the crime of dishonesty is too often unjustly laid."

TUCSON'S TOE TICKLER

A persistent itch was constantly irritating Jesus Cordova's mind. So, early on the morning of January 25, 1907, he did something to scratch it.

In the previous hours, Cordova had drunk far too many shots of mescal. According to the *Citizen*, Cordova thought "the sidewalk [was] rolling and tossing him about like a ship in a tempest." In his heavily inebriated state, Cordova stumbled along downtown's unpaved, dusty Jackson Street. The 100 block of the narrow lane was lined by eighteen adobe and fired-brick townhouses. Their front façades and entry doorways were immediately adjacent to the roadway, while a Chinese grocery, Yet Yuen Company's General Merchandise, was on the corner at south Meyer Street.

At 2:30 a.m., Cordova reached 112 West Jackson, a large adobe townhouse constructed by local businessman Mariano Samaniego around 1880. The home was occupied by a Syrian family, an exotic attraction in Tucson.

As he stood in front of the house, Cordova was seized by an overwhelming urge. "I just wanted to tickle their toes," he would later confess of the Syrians. Turning the handle on the door, Cordova found it unlocked and proceeded to enter the center hallway. His wobbly and disjointed steps woke and frightened a woman of the household, and as the *Citizen* reported, she "let out a piercing shriek that aroused the entire neighborhood." The woman's scream also soon brought policeman Carmen Mungia to the scene. Cordova was too far gone in his mescal-induced condition to run, so he simply slumped down in a chair. The officer arrested him for drunkenness and illegally entering a house. Taken to jail, Cordova pleaded guilty.

Later that day, hopefully having sobered up, Cordova stood in front of Recorder Judge Frank Treat. Believing the defendant's claim that he just wanted to tickle the Syrians' toes, he sentenced Cordova to fifteen days in the city jail, from which the prisoners were sent to do back-breaking road work.

Tucson's notorious Toe Tickler was almost assuredly one of the prisoners doing that hard labor. So maybe by the end of his jailhouse stay, Cordova would have lost his ticklish desire.

A SPECTACULAR FIRST

The Chinese men who began arriving in Tucson in the 1870s were either unmarried or had left wives behind in China, where they hoped to return one day. Because of the tiny number of Chinese women in Arizona, along with miscegenation laws, marriage for a single Chinese man was extremely difficult.

Despite those hurdles, eventually there were some Chinese weddings held at the joss house in Tucson's Chinatown. A 1908 Christian ceremony, however, gathered much more public attention. Jessie Goon was sixteen years old and marrying thirty-four-year-old Charles Gue. Jessie was the daughter of Lim Goon, a native of China, who was described as "one of the most prosperous Chinese merchants in the southwest." Both the bride and groom had been raised in Tucson, went to public schools and were Presbyterians. The marriage took place in two locations—first at the Odd Fellows Hall on east Congress Street and the following day at the joss house in Chinatown. It was reportedly the first Christian Chinese wedding in Tucson history.

Comparing the event to "a Fifth Avenue wedding on 'Gay Manhattan Isle,'" the *Star* indicated that three hundred people attended. Invitations, the newspaper wrote, "were lavishly issued and were in very large part [sent] to the prominent Americans and Mexicans of the city who are acquainted with the father of the bride."

Young Jessie wore "a magnificent white silk creation," as she walked down the aisle while her husband-to-be waited at the altar. Once their vows had been recited in front of Reverend W.W. Breckenridge, the couple exited the hall, and the *Star* stated, "It took two policemen to keep the sidewalk passably clear last night for the bride and groom to enter their carriage."

The festivities continued the next day at the joss house, where a Chinese feast for three hundred was served while the young bride poured tea. After that, the newlyweds moved to their house on south Meyer Street in Barrio Libre to begin life together.

Leaving an Impression

It was a warm May 1909 day. At the corner of Congress Street and Scott Avenue, an unnamed Papago woman was standing with a huge *olla*, or water jar, on her head. She wore a red calico skirt and a blue blouse of the same material, while her feet were in sandals.

For decades, tribal women had come into Tucson during the warm months to sell their earthen pottery. The labor required to make them, the *Citizen* stated, was extensive. Plus, to transport them, the women walked several miles all the way from the San Xavier Mission area with the *ollas* on their

Papago (Tohono O'odham) women made *ollas* for sale in territorial Tucson. *Library of Congress, photo no. 3c36586.*

heads. Yet they charged only one dollar or less for a large jar and half that much for a smaller one. "There is nothing quite like an olla to keep water cool on warm summer days," the *Citizen* acknowledged of their value. "They save ice and where ice is not to be had, are a great blessing."

The Papago woman on Congress Street asked a tall, silvery-haired man a question in her own language, which he did not comprehend. Seeking assistance, the elderly man inquired of a nearby Native American boy what the woman was saying. "Just wanted to know if her olla was on straight," was the honest reply.

MIXING IT UP

Annie Box wasn't afraid of a challenge. As a youngster, she both wrote music and played the piano at St. Joseph's Academy in downtown Tucson. Later, as a Black woman in territorial Arizona, she must have faced many other hurdles.

In her later years, Annie Box Neal still proudly displayed her rifle-toting abilities. *Arizona Historical Society, #58669.*

Having lived in Tucson since the early 1880s, Annie married William Neal, a prominent local businessman, in 1890. A few years later, north of town in Oracle, the couple opened the Mountain View Hotel, which was served by a daily stagecoach line. The twelve-room, two-story establishment cost $90,000 to build and had wraparound verandas on both floors. Each room, costing $2.50 a night or $12.50 for a week, came with hot and cold water along with a fireplace or stove. The *Star* wrote of the establishment, "Mr. and Mrs. Wm. Neal have spared neither pains nor expense in making this the most attractive hostelry in Arizona."

Annie grew her own vegetables to serve at hotel meals and presumably played the piano for her guests since there was a dance pavilion on the grounds. Once in a while, she would also ride by buckboard with her husband as he delivered gold bullion from the mining town of Mammoth to Tucson. For protection from bandits, she would tote along a long rifle and was said to be an excellent shot.

The hotel prospered and had famous guests, including entertainer William "Buffalo Bill" Cody and popular author Harold Bell Wright. Some of the customers came because they suffered from tuberculosis, and Oracle's cool, clear air was thought to be helpful in combating the disease.

While certainly dignified, Annie wasn't afraid to throw punches with men. Cowboys were employed at the Mountain View to watch over its herds of cattle, goats and pigs. On July 4, 1906, after they set off fireworks, some of the cowboys got drunk and started to fight in the hotel's kitchen. Annie tossed herself into the middle of the commotion and received a bloody nose as a reward.

After decades of managing the hotel, Annie died in 1950 at age eighty. Upon her death, it was written that she was "soft spoken and well educated." That she could mix it up with cowboys was an unacknowledged legacy.

Loyal Americans

When Confederates from Texas occupied Tucson in late February 1862, most of the "American" men in town, such as Granville H. Oury and Mark Aldrich, backed the rebellion. However, a few did not, including, most famously, Estevan Ochoa. Also remaining Union supporters were Charles Meyer and Theodore Mohrmann.

After the arrival of the Rebel soldiers—or "thugs," as thirty-seven-year-old German native Meyer referred to them—he was summoned to help raise their flag. "You give my compliments to the [Confederate] Captain," Meyer replied, "and tell him that we had already raised a [Union] flag and didn't need any other." The next day, Meyer was told that any more

Not everyone supported the Confederacy in 1862 Tucson; some people remained loyal to the Union. *Library of Congress, photo no. 3f03773.*

unacceptable backtalk would get him hanged, but he insisted, "I paid no attention to it at all."

About one month later, Meyer learned that Mohrmann was passing information to the Union army stationed at Yuma and would be strung up for his espionage. Meyer hurried off to tell Mohrmann, another native of Germany, what was planned for him. Mohrmann immediately gathered up as much cash as he could, bought a horse and saddle from Meyer and hightailed it south of the Mexican border.

For his part, Meyer soon afterward informed the Confederates that he wasn't hiding Mohrmann. The longtime local justice of the peace proudly recalled many years later that he then left town himself. Meyer went down toward the Mexican border to wait for Union troops to retake Tucson, something they eventually did. When that happened, territorial Tucson once again was both officially and practically part of the United States of America.

BIBLIOGRAPHY

Acknowledgements

Majewski, Teresita. "Memorial for James Edward (Jim) Ayres, 1936–2015." *Historical Archaeology* 49, no. 4 (2015): 1–11.

Chapter 1

Altshuler, Constance Wynn, ed. *Latest from Arizona: The Hesperian Letters, 1859–1861.* Tucson, AZ: Arizona Pioneers' Historical Society, 1969.

Carmony, Neil B., ed. *The Civil War in Apacheland.* Silver City, NM: High-Lonesome Books, 1996.

Congressional Globe. "A Century of Lawmaking for a New Nation: U.S. Congressional Documents and Debates, 1774–1875." Senate, 37th Congress, 3rd Session, 1,125–28, Library of Congress. www.memory.loc.gov.

Davis, Jefferson, to William Cannon, December 7, 1855. In *The Papers of Jefferson Davis.* Vol. 5. Baton Rouge: Louisiana State Press, 1985.

DeBow, J.D.B. "Commercial Spirit at the South." *Commercial Review* 2 (July 1846): 119–32.

Devine, David. *Slavery, Scandal, and Steel Rails: The 1854 Gadsden Purchase and the Building of the Second Transcontinental Railroad Across Arizona and New Mexico Twenty-Five Years Later.* New York: iUniverse, 2004.

Evening Star (Washington, D.C.). March 12, 1863.

Faust, David T., and Kenneth A. Randall. "Camp Lowell, and Tucson's Military Outpost, 1853–1873." *Smoke Signal*, no. 76 (Fall 2003): 130–32. Tucson Corral of the Westerners.

"Federal Census—Territories of New Mexico and Arizona, Excerpts from the Decennial Federal Census, 1860, for Arizona County in the Territory of New Mexico." Washington, D.C.: U.S. Government Printing Office, 1965.

"Federal Census—Territories of New Mexico and Arizona, Excerpts from the Special Territorial Census of 1864." Washington, D.C.: U.S. Government Printing Office, 1965.

Finch, L. Boyd. "Arizona in Exile: Confederate Schemes to Recapture the Far Southwest." *Journal of Arizona History* 33, no. 1 (Spring 1992): 65.

———. *Confederate Pathway to the Pacific: Major Sherod Hunter and Arizona Territory, C.S.A.* Tucson: Arizona Historical Society, 1996.

Journal of the Congress of the Confederate States of America, 1861–1865. Vol. 1. Washington, D.C.: U.S. Government Printing Office, 1904.

Lucero, Mrs. Carmen. 1928 oral interview. Arizona Historical Society Library, Tucson, Arizona.

Mesilla (NM) Times. June 30, 1861.

Morning Oregonian (Portland). February 28, 1862.

Nevada (CA) Democrat. November 9, 1859; September 5, 1861.

Oury, Granville H. *Alta California.* September 2, 1861. Granville H. Oury file of the Hayden Files, Arizona Historical Society Library, Tucson.

———. February 1862 letter to Provisional Congress from the State of Texas. Granville H. Oury file of the Hayden Files, Arizona Historical Society Library, Tucson.

Richmond Enquirer. January 18, 1854.

San Francisco Evening Bulletin. June 10, 1862.

Serven, James E. "The Military Posts on Sonoita Creek." *Smoke Signal*, no. 12 (Fall 1965): 37. Tucson Corral of the Westerners.

Sheridan, Thomas. *Los Tucsonenses: The Mexican Community in Tucson, 1854–1941.* Tucson: University of Arizona Press, 1986.

Thiel, J. Homer. "Uncovering the Presidio San Agustín del Tucson." *Smoke Signal*, no. 95 (December 2014): 103–4. Tucson Corral of the Westerners.

Weekly Union Record (Oroville, CA). July 29, 1865.

Wilson, John P. *When the Texans Came: Missing Records from the Civil War in the Southwest, 1861–1862.* Albuquerque: University of New Mexico Press, 2001.

Chapter 2

Arizona Citizen (Weekly). May 22, 1875; May 6, 1876; August 16, 1878; August 14, 1880; August 22, 1891; May 11, 1895; August 10, 1895.

Arizona Daily Star. October 12, 1907; August 10, 1909; April 25, 1911.

Arizona Star (Weekly). May 6, 1880; April 21, 1892; June 21, 1894; September 5, 1895.

Arizona State Board of Health. Original Certificate of Death for Gustavus Hollstein, September 5, 1919.

Daily Arizona Citizen/Tucson Citizen. September 24, 1887; April 16, 1889; January 11, 1894; April 16, 1894; August 31, 1895; September 28, 1897; March 18, 1907; November 9, 1907; November 11, 1907.

El Fronterizo (Tucson, AZ). September 3, 1892.

Weekly Arizonian (Tucson). April 8, 1871.

Chapter 3

Annie Londonderry. www.annielondonderry.com.

Arizona Citizen (Weekly). July 3, 1880; September 25, 1881; July 22, 1893; August 18, 1894; December 8, 1894; July 6, 1895.

Arizona Daily Star. July 9, 1879; September 30, 1879; September 10, 1887; July 15, 1902; June 19, 1907; October 27, 1907; March 10, 1908; August 3, 1908; October 24, 1908; October 16, 1909; May 3, 1910; June 5, 1910; March 19, 1911.

Arizona Republican (Phoenix). February 4, 1893.

Arizona Star (Weekly). June 23, 1892; February 9, 1893; September 14, 1893; May 24, 1894; June 14, 1894; August 16, 1894; November 29, 1894; June 20, 1895.

Biographical Directory of the United States Congress. "Oury, Granville Henderson." www.bioguide.congress.gov.

Caywood, W. Eugene, in collaboration with Keith Glaab, "Hooves & Rails: Tucson Street Railway, 1897–1906." Old Pueblo Trolley, 1998.

Daily Arizona Citizen/Tucson Citizen. April 5, 1880; September 30, 1880; July 29, 1882; September 23, 1882; April 2, 1885; July 15, 1885; August 4, 1906; August 11, 1906; October 4, 1906; September 2, 1907; May 5, 1910; June 11, 1910; June 23, 1910; January 2, 1911; April 27, 1976.

Devine, David. *Slavery, Scandal, and Steel Rails.* New York: iUniverse, 2004.

———. "Y19C." *Tucson Weekly*, December 23, 1999.

Dodge, Richard V. "San Diego's 'Impossible Railroad.'" Pacific Southwest Railway Museum Association. www.psrm.org.

Guroff, Margaret. *The Mechanical Horse: How the Bicycle Reshaped American Life.* Austin: University of Texas Press, 2016.

Herlihy, David V. "Crossroads in the Desert." *WUSTL Magazine* (August 2012). Washington University, St. Louis.

Jewish Women's Archive. "First Woman to Cycle the Globe Begins Journey." www.jwa.org/people.

Kalt, William D., III, and David Devine. "Tucson's Wondrous Railroad Depot: A History of the Toole Avenue Train Station." *Smoke Signal*, no. 88–89 (December 2010). Tucson Corral of the Westerners.

McCormick, Richard C. "Message of Governor McCormick to the Fifth Legislative Assembly of Arizona—Delivered at Tucson, November 16, 1868." History and Archives Division, Arizona Department of Library, Phoenix, Arizona.

Myrick, David. *Railroads of Arizona*. Vol. 1, *The Southern Roads*. Berkeley, CA: Howell-North Books, 1975.

New York Times. December 11, 2019.

Weekly Arizonian (Tucson). March 28, 1869; April 8, 1871.

Chapter 4

Arizona Citizen (Weekly). May 16, 1874; May 20, 1876; October 28, 1880; August 17, 1895.

Arizona Daily Star. June 29, 1884; November 11, 1886; February 10, 1911.

Arizona Silver Belt (Globe). October 30, 1880.

Arizona Star (Weekly). October 28, 1880; April 27, 1893; August 8, 1895; November 7, 1895.

Billman, Howard, Reverend, letter to Mrs. C.E. Walker, December 10, 1888. Tucson Indian Training School Records, MS 809, Arizona Historical Society Library, Tucson.

Daily Arizona Citizen/Tucson Citizen. May 23, 1885; August 22, 1889; April 22, 1891; May 6, 1901; May 7, 1901.

Devine, David. "President Rutherford B. Hayes Tours the Southwest Territories." *New Mexico Historical Review* 94, no. 1 (Winter 2019): 35–58.

———. "A Progressive Sweep." *Tucson Weekly*, December 8, 2011.

———. "Race to Washington: Why Arizona Is the Valentine's Day State." *Western Legal History* 26, nos. 1–2 (2013); 29–51.

Drachman, Mose. "Reminiscences." In Mose Drachman Papers, MS 0226, Box 44, File 552, Arizona Historical Society Library, Tucson.

El Fronterizo. October 31, 1880.

Fontana, Bernard L., and John P. Schaefer. *Of Earth and Little Rain: The Papago Indians.* Tucson: University of Arizona Press, 1981.

Holtby, David V. "Joint Statehood: A New Look at Before and After the 1906 Election." Paper presented at the joint Historical Convention of Arizona and New Mexico, April 2013.

Papago Tribe. "Tohono O'odham: History of the Desert People." University of Utah Printing Services, 1985. Available at the Arizona Historical Society Library, Tucson.

Pry, Mark E. "Statehood Politics and Territorial Development: The Arizona Constitution of 1891." *Journal of Arizona History* 35, no. 4 (Winter 1994): 397–426.

Ring Brothers Family History. "Tucson's Jewish Pioneers." www.ringbrothershistory.com.

Sheldon, Howard. "Camp Grant Massacre." Desert USA, www.desertusa.com.

Sheridan, Thomas. *Los Tucsonenses: The Mexican Community in Tucson, 1854–1941.* Tucson: University of Arizona Press, 1986.

Weekly Arizonian (Tubac). April 21, 1859.

Wikiwand. "San Carlos Apache Indian Reservation." https://www.wikiwand.com/en/San_Carlos_Apache_Indian_Reservation.

Chapter 5

Arizona Citizen (Weekly). July 8, 1876; July 15, 1876; September 16, 1876; December 2, 1876; April 19, 1884; March 19, 1887; October 21, 1893; May 19, 1894; April 4, 1896.

Arizona Daily Star. April 8, 1884; February 21, 1890; February 13, 1896; October 16, 1903; June 4, 1908; May 6, 1910; May 7, 1910; June 18, 1910; June 21, 1910; October 20, 1910; June 25, 1911; July 5, 1911; February 15, 1912.

Arizona Star (Weekly). April 9, 1885.

Carmony, Neil B., ed. *Whiskey, Six-Guns & Red-light Ladies: George Hand's Saloon Diary, Tucson, 1875–1878.* Silver City, NM: High-Lonesome Books, 1994.

Daily Arizona Citizen/Tucson Citizen. May 9, 1879; August 1, 1885; May 4, 1906; February 11, 1908; April 28, 1910; May 5, 1910; September 17, 1910.

El Fronterizo. May 11, 1879.

Erickson, Kirstin C. *Yaqui Homeland and Homeplace: The Everyday Production of Ethnic Identity*. Tucson: University of Arizona Press, 2008.

Gates, Henry Louis, Jr. "What Is Juneteenth?" PBS—African American History Blog. https://www.pbs.org/wnet/african-americans-many-rivers-to-cross/history/what-is-juneteenth.

Griffin-Pierce, Trudy. *Native Peoples of the Southwest*. Albuquerque: University of New Mexico Press, 2000.

Guidotti-Hernández, Nicole M. *Unspeakable Violence: Remapping U.S. and Mexican National Imaginaries*. Durham: Duke University Press, 2011.

Lawson, Harry. *The History of African-Americans in Tucson: An Afrocentric Perspective*. Vol. 1, *1860 to 1960*. Tucson, AZ: self-published, 1996.

Weekly Arizonian (Tucson). September 4, 1869.

Chapter 6

Arizona Citizen (Weekly). April 11, 1874; June 4, 1882; December 22, 1883.

Arizona Daily Star. June 28, 1879; July 30, 1879; February 7, 1883; February 24, 1897; January 25, 1898; September 23, 1902; February 25, 1903; February 16, 1905; April 21, 1905; October 17, 1905; December 30, 1906; January 30, 1907; August 23, 1907; December 27, 1907; March 18, 1908; October 24, 1908; April 8, 1909; May 12, 1909; August 19, 1909; December 8, 1910; December 11, 1910; March 1, 1911; June 29, 1911; September 15, 1911; October 10, 1911; November 5, 1911.

Arizona Star (Weekly). May 22, 1879; January 19, 1893; September 7, 1893; February 15, 1894; June 13, 1895; November 21, 1895; December 5, 1895; February 24, 1898; November 3, 1898.

Byrne, Leo G., and Sister Alberta Cammack. *Heritage: The Story of St. Mary's Hospital, 1880–1980*. Tucson, AZ: St. Mary's Hospital, 1981.

Corrigan, Sister Monica. *Trek of the Seven Sisters*. Tucson, AZ: Carondelet Health Network, 1997.

Daily Arizona Citizen/Tucson Citizen. April 9, 1879; September 8, 1879; July 1, 1880; July 16, 1880; September 26, 1885; February 14, 1887; May 14, 1900; March 6, 1903; December 8, 1903; December 7, 1905; December 30, 1908; April 18, 1910; July 27, 1910; October 29, 1910; May 1, 1911.

Devine, David. *The St. Luke's in the Desert Story: A Century of Community Service*. Tucson, AZ: St. Luke's in the Desert, 2018.

Hall, Dick. "Ointment of Love: Oliver E. Comstock and Tucson's Tent City." *Journal of Arizona History* 19, no. 2 (Summer 1978): 111–30.

Pima County Medical Society. "A Brief Look at Southern Arizona Medical History and the Pima County Medical Society." www.pimamedicalsociety.org/about-us/history.

United States Census for Tucson, Arizona, 1860, 1870, 1880.

Women's Plaza of Honor, The University of Arizona. "Dr. Rosa Meador Goodrich Boido." www.plaza.sbs.arizona.edu.

Chapter 7

Arizona Capitol Times (Phoenix). March 13, 1985.

Arizona Citizen (Weekly). December 10, 1870; December 21, 1872; December 3, 1882; June 7, 1884; December 9, 1893; December 30, 1893; December 8, 1894; April 27, 1895.

Arizona Daily Star. August 15, 1879; September 8, 1897; June 23, 1904; July 14, 1907; December 17, 1907; September 20, 1908; September 7, 1909; September 30, 1909; December 9, 1909; February 19, 1910; January 14, 1911; April 30, 1911; May 7, 1911; November 12, 1911; April 25, 1943.

Arizona Star (Weekly). May 12, 1892; August 24, 1893; October 26, 1893; January 11, 1894; May 16, 1895; August 24, 1899; October 5, 1899.

Chanin, Abe. *They Fought Like Wildcats*. Tucson, AZ: Midbar Press, 1979.

Daily Arizona Citizen/Tucson Citizen. June 30, 1879; November 14, 1879; December 1, 1879; June 25, 1880; July 7, 1880; December 11, 1880; December 11, 1882; March 12, 1885; February 9, 1886; April 18, 1887; July 21, 1897; February 6, 1902; March 23, 1903; April 11, 1906; July 15, 1907; October 9, 1907; February 8, 1909; April 16, 1910; May 17, 1910; July 5, 1910; August 8, 1910; September 3, 1910; July 24, 1911.

Herring Hall. "History." www.cals.arizona.edu/herringhall/history.

Leighton, David. "Oracle Road Strip Mall Site Was Tucson's First Amusement Park." *Arizona Daily Star*, December 2, 2014.

———. "Tucson's Park Avenue Named for Sports Venue." *Arizona Daily Star*, January 19, 2015.

Riffe, Terri Dean. "A History of Women's Sports at the University of Arizona." PhD diss., University of Arizona, 1986.

Ring Brothers Family History. "Tucson's Jewish Pioneers." www.ringbrothershistory.com.

Svob, Robert S. "History of Intercollegiate Athletics at the University of Arizona (1897–1948)." MA thesis, University of Arizona, 1950.

Weekly Arizonian (Tucson). December 31, 1870.

Chapter 8

Arizona Citizen (Weekly). October 25, 1879; May 8, 1881; January 22, 1882; August 29, 1885.

Arizona Daily Star. July 9, 1879; June 24, 1897; February 4, 1898; June 20, 1907; August 28, 1907; March 17, 1908; March 20, 1908; March 31, 1908; August 16, 1908; September 27, 1908; December 23, 1908; February 19, 1909; December 4, 1909; April 28, 1910; October 4, 1910; November 13, 1910; April 4, 1911.

Arizona Star (Weekly). May 3, 1883; July 14, 1887; February 5, 1891; August 20, 1891; January 19, 1893; April 6, 1893; May 4, 1899; September 14, 1899.

Bufkin, Don. "From Mud Village to Modern Metropolis: The Urbanization of Tucson." *Journal of Arizona History* 22, no. 2 (Spring 1981): 63–98.

A Centennial History of the First Congregational Church, United Church of Christ, Tucson, Arizona, 1881–1981. Balkow Graphic Sales, November 22, 1981.

Daily Arizona Citizen/Tucson Citizen. August 2, 1879; October 18, 1886; September 24, 1904; September 21, 1905; April 6, 1906; October 8, 1906; January 25, 1907; January 23, 1908; May 17, 1909; September 6, 1910; January 7, 1911; August 31, 1911; October 5, 1911; November 14, 1911.

El Fronterizo. May 9, 1884.

"History of Christian Science in Tucson." Christian Science ephemera file, Arizona Historical Society Library, Tucson.

Ho, Chuimei, and Bennet Bronson. "The Chee Kung Tong: A Chinese Secret Society in Tucson, 1880–1940." *Journal of Arizona History* 59, no. 1 (Spring 2018): 6.

Sheridan, Thomas. *Los Tucsonenses: The Mexican Community in Tucson, 1854–1941.* Tucson: University of Arizona Press, 1986.

Stephenson, Patricia Peters. *Trial and Triumph: The Life and Accomplishments of Louise Foucar Marshall.* Tucson, AZ: self-published, 2015.

Stewart, Janet Ann. "The Mansions of Main Street." *Journal of Arizona History* 20, no. 2 (Summer 1979): 193–222.

Tucson City Council minutes, March 21, 1910. City Clerk's Office, Tucson, Arizona.

Tucson City Directory. Tucson: Arizona Directory Company, 1912.

Wallace, Jerry. "The Episcopal Church Comes to Arizona." N.p.: Grace Episcopal Church, 1974.

Weekly Arizonian (Tubac). March 10, 1859.

Wilson, Bernard. "20th Century Tucson's Black Residents Map." Arizona Historical Society Library, Tucson, 2008.

Chapter 9

Arizona Citizen (Weekly). September 27, 1873; October 22, 1882; March 22, 1884; November 14, 1885; December 3, 1892; July 7, 1894.

Arizona Daily Star. July 10, 1879; July 15, 1879; August 1, 1879; March 28, 1885; October 21, 1885; February 26, 1887; March 26, 1901; April 27, 1902; April 28, 1904; July 18, 1907; September 5, 1907; March 18, 1908; May 6, 1908; February 18, 1909; February 18, 1910; March 29, 1911; April 16, 1911; April 26, 1933.

Arizona Star (Weekly). November 25, 1880; October 27, 1881; January 4, 1883; July 28, 1892; October 27, 1892; February 1, 1894; December 29, 1898; April 6, 1899.

Daily Arizona Citizen/Tucson Citizen. March 17, 1879; March 2, 1880; March 9, 1880; June 2, 1880; November 22, 1880; December 31, 1880; December 9, 1882; March 19, 1885; June 6, 1885; June 8, 1885; May 12, 1886; April 12, 1887; July 15, 1898; April 23, 1904; August 9, 1904; May 4, 1905; January 18, 1906; January 29, 1906; March 15, 1906; March 27, 1906; March 28, 1906; March 29, 1906; March 30, 1906; August 8, 1906; December 14, 1906; December 31, 1906; April 2, 1907; May 3, 1911; May 4, 1911; September 1, 1911.

Devine, David. "From Railroad to Warehouse: The Story of the Northside of Tucson's Downtown." *Smoke Signal*, no. 64 (Fall 1995). Tucson Corral of the Westerners.

———. *Tucson: A History of the Old Pueblo from the 1854 Gadsden Purchase.* Jefferson, NC: McFarland & Company, 2015.

Kalt, William D., III. *High in Desert Skies: Early Arizona Aviation.* Arizona: William Kalt Books, 2017.

Lyons, Betina. *Zeckendorfs and Steinfelds: Merchant Princes of the American Southwest.* Tucson: Arizona Historical Society, 2008.

Schneider, Gus. *George Hands Tucson: 1870–1880.* Map, 1941. Arizona Historical Society Library, Tucson.

Weekly Arizonian (Tucson). January 22, 1870.

Chapter 10

Arizona Citizen (Weekly). November 17, 1883.

Arizona Daily Star. September 9, 1903; March 28, 1908; March 29, 1908; June 13, 1908; April 2, 1910; April 3, 1910; January 5, 1948.

Box, Annie M., and William Neal. Marriage Certificate dated June 26, 1890. Ancestry.com. www.ancestrylibrary.com.

Daily Arizona Citizen/Tucson Citizen. June 3, 1890; March 7, 1904; November 19, 1904; April 13, 1905; April 25, 1905; January 25, 1907; March 28, 1908; May 11, 1909; July 2, 1910; February 3, 1911; March 19, 1912.

Delanti, Francisca, Maria Gomallanes and Dolores Salazar. 1910 census information. Ancestry.com. www.ancestrylibrary.com.

Devine, David. "Portraits from the Past." *Tucson Weekly*, February 20, 2003.

El Fronterizo. January 12, 1889.

Finch, L. Boyd. *Confederate Pathway to the Pacific: Major Sherod Hunter and Arizona Territory, C.S.A.* Tucson: Arizona Historical Society, 1996.

Goon, Jessie, and Charles Gue. Arizona select marriages, 1888–1908. Ancestry.com. www.ancestrylibrary.com.

Hilzinger, John George. "Churches." *Treasure Land.* Arizona: Arizona Advancement Company, 1897.

Lijero, Pablo. 1885–1940 Indian Census Rolls information. Ancestry.com. www.ancestrylibrary.com.

Mohrmann, Theodore. Information in Hayden file, Arizona Historical Society Library, Tucson.

Old Pueblo Club Chronicle. October 1979. Arizona Historical Society Library, Tucson.

Pomroy, Nellie. Last will and testament, 1923. Ancestry.com. www.ancestrylibrary.com.

———. 1913 voting registration data. Window On Your Past. windowonyourpast.com/site/research/arizona-suffrage/1913-women-voters-data.

Tucson City Directory, 1912. Arizona Historical Society Library, Tucson.

Tucson Library Directors. www.library.pima.gov.

Weekly Arizonian (Tucson). June 26, 1869.

Wilson, Bernard. *The Black Residents of Tucson and Their Achievements, 1860–1900: A Reference Guide.* Self-published, 2007. Arizona Historical Society Library, Tucson.

INDEX

D

E

F

G

N

O

P

R

S

ABOUT THE AUTHOR

A 1975 graduate of the University of Arizona with an MS degree in urban planning, David Devine and his wife, Susie Morris, returned to Tucson in 1980. He soon became involved with historic preservation efforts in the central city. Beginning in 1995, he began writing about Tucson and southern Arizona history. Since then, he has authored two books and seven monographs on those subjects. He also wrote numerous articles on local history for the *Tucson Weekly*, for which he was a frequent contributor from 1995 until his retirement in 2011.